SCHOOL LAW CASEBOOK SERIES—NO. 7

The Law Governing School Property and School-Building Construction

By
LEE O. GARBER

and

NEWTON EDWARDS

The Interstate
Printers and Publishers
Danville, Illinois

CONTENTS

Page

Introduction vii

Authors' Preface viii

I. Legal Principles................................... 1
   Ownership and Control of School Property........ 3
   Acquisition and Location of School Sites.......... 4
   Employment of Architects...................... 5
   Bids on Building Contracts..................... 6
   Illegal and Void Building Contracts............. 7
   Ratification of School-Building Contracts......... 7
   Defective Performance of Building Contracts...... 8
   Contractors' Bonds............................. 8

II. Court Decisions................................. 11
   1. *Pritchett* v. *County Board of School Trustees*.... 13
   2. *Ross* v. *Adams Mills Rural School District*....... 14
   3. *Salt Lake City* v. *Board of Education of Salt Lake
      City* 16
   4. *Nelson* v. *Mayor etc. of Town of Homer*........ 18
   5. *State* v. *Zeidler*............................ 19
   6. *State ex rel. Clark* v. *Haworth*................ 21
   7. *City of Bloomfield* v. *Davis County Community
      School District* 22
   8. *Community Fire Protection District of St. Louis
      County* v. *Board of Education*.............. 24
   9. *Nichols* v. *School Directors*.................... 27
   10. *Southside Estates Baptist Church* v. *Board of
       Trustees* 29
   11. *Spencer* v. *Joint School District*............... 31
   12. *Williams* v. *McKenzie*....................... 32
   13. *State* v. *Board of Education*................... 34
   14. *Reiger* v. *Board of Education*.................. 35
   15. *Maxcy* v. *City of Oshkosh*.................... 37
   16. *State* v. *Stojack*............................. 39
   17. *Sargent* v. *Town of Merrimac*................. 40

18. *Mulligan* v. *School District* 42
19. *Consolidated School District* v. *Walter* 43
20. *Washington City Board of Education* v. *Edgerton* 46
21. *Scott County Board of Education* v. *Pepper* 47
22. *Harris* v. *Consolidated School District* 49
23. *Pike County Board of Education* v. *Ford* 51
24. *Sarratt* v. *Cash* 52
25. *People ex rel. Kiehm* v. *Board of Education* 54
26. *Cobb* v. *Pasadena City Board of Education* 55
27. *Dierks Special School District* v. *Van Dyke* 56
28. *Pierce* v. *Board of Education* 58
29. *Fiske* v. *School District* 60
30. *Ritter* v. *School District* 61
31. *Page* v. *Harlingen Independent School District* .. 62
32. *Smith* v. *Board of Education* 64
33. *Coward* v. *Mayor, etc., of City of Bayonne* 65
34. *Yoder* v. *School District of Luzerne Township* ... 67
35. *Reams* v. *Cooley* 69
36. *Homan* v. *Board of Education* 70
37. *Meyer* v. *Board of Education* 71
38. *Joseph Rugo, Inc.* v. *Henson* 73
39. *Wayne Crouse, Inc.* v. *School District of*
      Borough of Braddock 75
40. *Board of Education* v. *Hooper* 76
41. *Hibbs* v. *Arensberg* 78
42. *Honey Creek School Township* v. *Barnes* 79
43. *White River School Township* v. *Dorrell* 81
44. *School Directors* v. *Fogelman* 82
45. *Sullivan* v. *School District* 84
46. *Frank* v. *Board of Education of Jersey City* 85
47. *State* v. *Goodman* 87
48. *Dodge* v. *Kimball* 89
49. *Rubino* v. *Board of Trustees* 91
50. *Board of President and Directors of the St. Louis*
      Public Schools v. *Woods* 93
51. *Dunlap* v. *Eden* 94
52. *Phoenix Indemnity Co.* v. *Board of Public*
      Instruction 96

53. *Blyth-Fargo Co. v. Free* 97
54. *Independent District of Mason City v. Reichard* .. 99
55. *Maryland Casualty Co. v. Eagle River Union Free High School District* 100
56. *United States Fidelity & Guaranty Co. v. Cicero Smith Lumber Co.* 102
57. *Collins v. National Fire Insurance Company of Hartford* 103
58. *Tennessee Supply Company v. Bina Young & Son* 105
59. *Green Bay Lumber Co. v. Independent School District* 107
60. *Levinson v. Linderman* 109
61. *Freeman v. City of Chanute* 111
62. *Plumbing Supply Co. v. Board of Education* 112
63. *Warren v. Glens Falls Indemnity Co.* 114
Selected Bibliography 116

INTRODUCTION

This casebook takes its place as the third in the second series of four books which, taken together, may be thought of as giving coverage to the field of "School Law." The earlier books in this series are "The Law Governing School Board Members and School Board Meetings" and "Tort and Contractual Liability of School Districts and School Boards." One more will follow. It will deal with School Finance.

Professors of School Law, who are seeking new and practical materials and who are desirous of using the case method of teaching, will welcome these casebooks as unique aids. Likewise, professors of Educational Administration who are interested in supplementing their instructional materials with additional materials of a legal nature should find these books exceedingly helpful.

The authors are well known for their work in this field—School Law. Newton Edwards is the author of the well-known textbook and reference work—*The Courts and the Public Schools*. Lee O. Garber is the author of *The Yearbook of School Law*, an annual publication since 1950. He has also been a regular contributor to *The Nation's Schools* since 1951.

Russell L. Guin,
Editor

Authors' Preface

This casebook follows the familiar pattern which characterizes the six that preceded it. It has two main sections—"Legal Principles" and "Court Decisions." From the legal principles mentioned in the first section, the most significant are selected and illustrated with appropriate court decisions in the second section.

The first four casebooks were designed to give coverage to the first half of a comprehensive course in School Law. This is the third in a projected series of four designed to give coverage to the last half of the School Law course.

The legal principles are selective and not exhaustive. Many of the cases selected illustrate more than one legal principle. Therefore, an instructor may become even more selective in his choice of cases for his class to consider if time is a matter of critical import.

It must be remembered that there is not, necessarily, uniformity of agreement among the courts on all questions. Courts deviate and, in the case of the most important deviations, court decisions are chosen to illustrate both points of view.

In addition to professors of School Law and School Administration, it is hoped that these casebooks will prove of both interest and value to practicing school administrators and school-board solicitors or attorneys.

Lee O. Garber
Newton Edwards

I.

LEGAL PRINCIPLES

The Law Governing School Property and School-Building Construction

Ownership and Control of School Property

Inasmuch as public education is a state function, public school property is state property held in trust for the state by local school authorities. It follows that the transfer of school property from one district to another by virtue of statutory authority does not deprive a school district or its inhabitants of property without due process of law. Whatever authority a school board may have over school property is authority which has been conferred upon it by statute.

Since education is a state and not a municipal function, cities and towns, even though they occupy the same territory as school districts, possess no inherent control over public schools; such authority as they may exercise over public schools and the buildings in which they are housed must be expressly and clearly conferred upon them by charter or statute. Cities and towns, unless authorized by statute, may not expend municipal funds for the construction of school buildings. Municipal officers have no inherent authority to control or manage school property. And this is true where a home-rule charter confers upon the city authority to regulate its local affairs. This follows from the fact that education is a state and not a local affair. A number of courts have held that school property is state property, subject to the exercise of the police power of the state residing in its local school boards; and the municipal authorities may not, therefore, require local school boards to obey their building ordinances or codes. But in some cases the courts have held that the police power of the municipality takes precedence over the police power of the school board where safety and sanitation are concerned.

State legislatures may authorize school boards to permit the use of school property for any purpose not prohibited by the constitution, and in a number of states the courts have sustained statutes authorizing a wide use of school buildings. In the absence of statutes authorizing the use of school buildings for other than school purposes, state courts have differed widely in their rulings. Some have

3

permitted the use of schoolhouses for religious meetings of one kind or another provided there was no interference with the regular work of the school, but others have held that no kind of religious exercises could be held in a schoolhouse unless specifically authorized by statute. The courts have been divided, too, on such matters as the authority of school boards to permit the use of school buildings for social and political meetings or to lease school property for a private or commercial purpose. For example, they have approved the leasing of school property for the drilling of oil and gas, although the opposite has also been held.

Acquisition and Location of School Sites

As a rule, school boards are vested with specific statutory authority to acquire school sites, but even in the absence of such authority the courts hold that authority to build school buildings carries with it, by necessary implication, authority to purchase school sites. Authority to purchase school sites carries with it by implication authority to purchase the necessary playgrounds and athletic fields, and these do not have to be adjacent to the lot on which the schoolhouse is situated. School boards are vested with authority to accept donations of property to be used for school purposes, but when school boards accept such a donation they will be required to administer it perpetually according to the terms of the donor.

School boards, under statutory authority, may take private property by the exercise of the right of eminent domain; and, when they do so, the courts will permit them a wide exercise of discretion both with respect to the need of taking the property and the amount to be taken. When property is taken by the right of eminent domain, the courts will require the board to pay the owner a fair market price for the property when put to its most profitable use; the owner of land taken by eminent domain must be compensated for whatever loss he suffers. When land is taken by eminent domain, the fee remains with the original owner, unless the statutes provide otherwise, and when the property is no longer used for school purposes it reverts to the original owner.

When property is conveyed to a school board and the deed clearly provides for the reversion of the property to the original owner when no longer used for school purposes, the board does not own the property in fee simple, and it reverts to the original owner or his heirs when no longer used for school purposes. But the courts do not look with favor on deeds that provide for reverter of school property, and such deeds will be construed strictly against the grantor. Where property was deeded to school districts "for school purposes only," "so long as the property shall be used for school purposes and no longer," or "to be used for school property in perpetuity," courts have held that the property did not revert to the grantor when no longer used for school purposes. Before a court will declare a forfeiture, it must be very clear that school authorities intended to abandon the use of property for school purposes. It has been held that property is no longer used for school purposes when it has been sold or leased and the proceeds are being used to maintain a school.

In the exercise of its discretion to select school sites, a school board will not have its discretion controlled by the courts so long as it is exercised in good faith and not abused. A school board must be free to exercise its discretion and best judgment at the time it makes the determination of a school site; it cannot limit its discretion in this respect by prior commitments or understandings with the public.

Employment of Architects

Authority of a school board to build school buildings carries with it, by implication, authority to employ architects. In employing an architect, a school board need not resort to competitive bidding in the absence of statute to the contrary. Contracts with architects, like all other contracts, must be made by the board in its corporate capacity and not by an individual member or committee of the board. It is well settled that, where an architect agrees to furnish plans and specifications for a building that can be built at a cost closely approximating a given amount, or not to exceed a certain sum, he cannot recover under the contract unless the building he designs can be erected for the sum stipulated, or unless the increased cost is due to some special circumstance. Some courts hold—and their decisions appear to be the most reasonable—that a contract between a school board and an architect to prepare general drawings and specifications for a school building is valid even though the board may not, at the time, have the necessary funds to build the building and the building may never be built. These courts reason that the plans and specifications of the architect are necessary to enable the school board to determine what the kind of building desired would cost; even if the projected building is never erected, the architect's fee would be chargeable to the general fund. Some courts take the position, however, that a contract between a school board and an architect is invalid where the plans and specifications call for a building which would cost more than the board could legally spend for that purpose.

Where a school board breaks a contract with an architect, the rule is that he is entitled to recover the contract price, less whatever payments have been made and less what it would cost him to perform the contract.

Bids on Building Contracts

Where the statutes do not require school boards to let building contracts on the basis of competitive bidding, a school board may or may not, at its discretion, advertise for bids. And in such cases, the board may reject all bids unless its advertisement is so worded as to constitute an offer to accept the lowest bid. In case the statutes require school boards to advertise for bids on school-building contracts and to award such contracts to the lowest responsible bidder, the mode of making the contract is the measure of the board's power to make it, and if the statute is disregarded, the contractor cannot recover on the contract. As a rule, under such circumstances, the contractor cannot recover on *quantum meruit*, in a court of equity, the actual value of the building. In order to have competitive bidding, plans and specifications must be sufficiently definite to enable those who bid to bid on a common basis; otherwise there is no competition. A school board may ask for bids on alternate plans and proposals, and there is competitive bidding even though only one bid is received. Where the statutes require that bids be let to the lowest responsible bidder, in deciding who is the lowest responsible bidder, the board should take into consideration cost, financial standing, experience, resources, and all other factors necessary for it to form a judgment on the bidder's responsibility. Where a school board acts in good faith and its judgment is based upon substantial fact, the courts will not overrule its discretion in determining the lowest responsible bidder. The mere passage of a resolution by a board to accept a bid does not constitute a contract—there is no contract until the bidder has been officially notified that his bid has been accepted—and a board may rescind its resolution awarding the contract at any time before such notification. If a contractor makes an honest mistake in calculating the cost of a school building and the mistake goes to the essence of the contract, a court of equity will annul the bid and put the parties *in statu quo*. After bids have been accepted, courts will permit minor, but not major, changes in the specifications; to permit major changes would be equivalent to letting a new contract without competitive bidding.

Illegal and Void Building Contracts

School boards have only such powers as are conferred upon them by statute; when a school board enters into a contract for the purchase of school property in excess of its statutory authority, the contract is *ultra vires*. In some states a school district will not be bound under an *ultra vires* contract even though it retains and enjoys the use of property obtained under such a contract. The courts in some states, however, hold that a district must pay for property retained and used under an *ultra vires* contract.

Ratification of School-Building Contracts

If a school board makes a contract for the erection of a school building or for the purchase of other school property which it had no authority to make, it cannot later ratify the contract by any act of its own so as to make it binding on the board. But if a school board enters into a contract for the purchase of school property which it had authority to make and the contract is unenforceable because of some irregularity in the making of it, the board may later ratify it. Formal action to ratify is not necessary; ratification takes place when a board so acts that its action is incompatible with any other assumption than its intent to ratify.

Defective Performance of Building Contracts

A school board may not refuse to accept a schoolhouse if the contractor has acted in good faith and substantially performed his contract. It is difficult to determine what constitutes substantial performance of a building contract but the courts are agreed that there is no substantial performance unless the building is such as to accomplish the purpose for which it was built. Where there is substantial performance, a board will be required to pay the contractor the contract price, less deductions to cover omissions in performance. Even though a school building has been accepted and paid for, it has been held that a school board may sue the contractor for defective performance.

Contractors' Bonds

Authority to build schoolhouses carries with it by implication authority to require a contractor to whom a building contract is let to give a bond guaranteeing the faithful performance of the contract and the payment for all labor and materials used in the construction of the building. As a rule, the obligation of a surety on a bond to insure the performance of a building contract is measured by the terms of the contract; but where the liability in the contract is broader than in the bond, many courts have held that the bond is the measure of the surety's liability. An accommodation surety—one who receives no pay—is a favorite of the law, and if there is any doubt with respect to the obligations under the bond it will be resolved in his favor; but contracts for suretyship will be construed more strictly against a surety for pay. When the bond is given by a surety company for pay, the bond is interpreted as are other contracts with a view of giving effect to the true meaning of the parties. Under the common law it was originally held that any change in a contract without the consent of the surety released the surety from all liability. With the rise of bonding companies for pay, however, the rule has been changed, and now it is generally held that the surety will be relieved entirely only if the change in the contract increases his liability materially; and, if the change is not great enough to relieve the surety entirely, he will be relieved *pro tanto—i.e.,* to the amount of his extra obligation.

A surety who gives a bond guaranteeing the performance of a building contract and the payment for labor and materials will not be relieved of his obligation to laborers and materialmen by any alteration in the original contract to which they did not give their consent. In a number of states the statutes require a contractor to give a bond to pay for labor and materials. Where there is evidence from surrounding circumstances or some provision in the bond that the contractor intended to give a statutory bond, the terms of the statute will generally be read into the bond and the surety will be held liable to pay for labor and materials. But other courts interpret the bond strictly and will not read the terms of the statute into it. Where a contractor agrees to provide the labor and materials used in the construction of a school building and gives a bond to guarantee that his contract will be performed, he does not definitely agree to pay for the labor and materials, and there is no right of action against his surety. Where a contract to construct a school building provides that the board retain each month a certain percentage of what is due the contractor in order to insure the completion of the building, and the contractor defaults, the contractor's surety has a claim on the retained percentage superior to that of laborers and materialmen or of a bank to which the contractor has assigned his rights to the retained percentage.

It is commonly held that a school district will not be held liable for failure to take a bond conditioned to pay for labor and materials even though a statute requires that such a bond be taken. Where the statutes require a school board to take a bond conditioned to pay for labor and materials going into the construction of a school building, members of the board will not, as a rule, be held personally liable for failure to take such a bond, although the opposite has been held.

II.

COURT DECISIONS

Court Decisions

1. *"Inasmuch as public education is a state function, public property is state property held in trust for the state by local school authorities" (p. 3).*

Pritchett v. County Board of School Trustees,
5 Ill. (2d) 356, 125 N.E. (2d) 476 (1955)
(Decided by the Supreme Court of Illinois)

[This was an action involving the constitutionality of certain statutes relating to the reorganization of school districts. In arriving at its decision, the court found it necessary to comment on the legal status of school property.]

Dailey, Justice.

. . . .

A frequently cited proposition is that the State may, with or without the consent of the inhabitants of a school district, or against their protest, and with or without notice or hearing, take the school facilities in the district without compensation and vest them in other districts or agencies. The State may hold or manage the facilities directly or indirectly. The area of the district may be contracted or expanded, it may be divided, united in whole or in part with another district, and the district may be abolished. All this at the will of the legislature. The "property of the school district" is a phrase which is misleading. The district owns no property, all school facilities, such as grounds, buildings, equipment, etc., being in fact and law the property of the State and subject to the legislative will.

Guides for Class Discussion

1. Compare this decision with the one in *Ross* v. *Adams Mills Rural School District, infra.*
2. Do you agree with the court? Give reasons.

2. "... *the transfer of school property from one district to another by virtue of statutory authority does not deprive a school district or its inhabitants of property without due process of law*" (p. 3).

Ross v. Adams Mills Rural School District,
113 Ohio St. 466, 149 N.E. 634 (1925)
(Decided by the Supreme Court of Ohio)

[When part of one rural district that had a bonded indebtedness was transferred to a second rural district, the second district was ordered to pay $25,000 toward the reduction of the indebtedness of the first district. The second district refused to do so, but the county auditor levied the tax on all the property of the district. To enjoin the levy and collection of the tax, this action was brought. The court refused to enjoin the levy and collection. In arriving at its decision the court saw fit to comment on the effect of a statute that provided for the transfer of school property from one district to another.]

Matthias, J. . . .

. . . .

It seems to be the clear purpose and intent of the provisions of section 4692, General Code, to require that any of the indebtedness of the district from which territory is transferred shall be apportioned between the districts from which and to which such territory is transferred. Indeed, it is impossible to make that provision of the statute effective if not so interpreted and applied.

When such division was made the indebtedness became the indebtedness of the Adams Mills district and of the Jefferson district, as apportioned. Under the provisions of section 4692, General Code, the "legal title of the property of the board of education shall become vested in the board of education of the school district to which such property is transferred," and, when an equitable division of the indebtedness was made, all the property in each district became liable for its respective proportion thereof. There is no statutory provision which would authorize a tax levied upon only a portion of a district or subdivision and no method has been prescribed, and none has been suggested, whereby that could be done. It would be contrary to the provisions of all tax levying and tax limitation statutes. In accordance with the familiar principles of statutory construction, section 4692, General Code, will be so construed as to make it a valid enactment for all purposes, and proceedings thereunder will, if possible, be so construed as to accomplish a valid result. Just as legislation enacted subsequent to the issuance of bonds that would remove a portion of the security thereof, and thereby impair the obligation of contract, would be invalid as against the holders of said bonds so also would a proceeding under this statute which undertook to transfer a portion of the district be a nullity against holders of the bonds, if it did not provide for the apportionment of the indebtedness and payment of the bonds as contemplated in the original proceeding for the issuance thereof, as required by the constitutional and statutory provisions heretofore referred to.

The contention that such statutory provision is violative of the due process clause of the federal Constitution has been considered in numerous cases and decided adversely thereto. In Hunter v. City of Pittsburgh, 207 U. S. 161, 28 S. Ct. 40, 52 L. Ed. 151, it was held:

"There is no contract, within the meaning of the contract clause of the Federal Constitution, between a municipality and its citizens and taxpayers that the latter shall be taxed only for the uses of that corporation and not for the uses of any like corporation with which it may be consolidated."

The language of Justice Moody, who rendered the opinion of the court, is pertinent here. After referring to the powers conferred upon municipal corporations and their status as political subdivisions of the state, he said, at page (28 S. Ct. 46):

"The State, therefore, at its pleasure may modify or withdraw all such powers, may take without compensation such property, hold it itself, or vest it in other agencies, expand or contract the territorial area, unite the whole or a part of it with another municipality, repeal the charter and destroy the corporation. . . . Although the inhabitants and property owners may by such changes suffer inconvenience, and their property may be lessened in value by the burden of increased taxation, or for any other reason, they have no right by contract or otherwise in the unaltered or continued existence of the corporation or its powers, and there is nothing in the federal Constitution which protects them from these injurious consequences."

Guides for Class Discussion

1. Do you think the court's decision was equitable? Give reasons.
2. What is meant by the due-process-of-law clause?
3. Had there been no statute governing the matter, what rule would the court have undoubtedly followed?
4. Compare the decision in this case with that rendered in *Pritchett* v. *County Board of School Trustees, supra.*

3. "Since . . . *cities and towns . . . possess no inherent control over public schools, such authority as they may exercise over public schools and the buildings in which they are housed must be expressly and clearly conferred upon them by charter or statute*" (p. 3).

SALT LAKE CITY v. BOARD OF EDUCATION OF SALT LAKE CITY,
52 Utah 540, 175 P. 654 (1918)
(Decided by the Supreme Court of Utah)

[This action was brought by a city to enjoin a board of education from proceeding further in the construction of a school building. It was contended that, because the building did not meet the requirements of certain building ordinances, the district could not erect it. The lower court ruled for the city and enjoined the district. On appeal the higher court reversed the lower court. It held that, in the absence of authority granted it by statute, the municipality had no control over the public schools.]

FRICK, C. J. . . .

.   .   .   .

The contention of appellants' counsel can perhaps be best stated in their own language as contained in their printed brief. They say:

"The question for decision is as to whether the plaintiff city, acting in pursuance of the police powers conferred upon it by general law, may impose building restrictions or regulations upon the defendant board of education in the erection of school buildings. . . .

.   .   .   .

Respondent's counsel . . . contend that the power of police regulation is exclusively vested in the cities and that the boards of education possess no such power. . . .

.   .   .   .

. . . the mere fact that no police powers are vested in the boards of education [is not] decisive of the question of whether the state has in fact surrendered to the cities plenary police power over our public school buildings.

. . . Counsel for respondent insist that such power is clearly conferred in the several subdivisions of [the statute]. . . . A careful reading and consideration, however, of the provisions contained in [these] subdivisions . . . in our judgment clearly shows that it was not the intention of the Legislature to make those provisions applicable to public school buildings. . . .

.   .   .   .

In connection with the principles just quoted, another one must not be overlooked which is admirably expressed by the Court of Appeals of Kentucky in the case of Kentucky Institution for Education of Blind v. City of Louisville, 123 Ky. 767, 97 S.W. 402, 8 L. R. A. (N. S.) 533, in the following words:

"The principle is that the state, when creating municipal governments, does not cede to them any control of the state's property situated within them, nor over any property which the state has authorized another body or power to control."

.   .   .   .

. . . In this connection it is perhaps but just and fair to counsel for respondent to state that they concede that the ordinances of respondent would have no application to what they call state buildings, although such buildings are located within the limits of the city. This concession is made in deference to the principle quoted from the Kentucky case to which we have referred. Under our Constitution and statutes, however, we can conceive of no distinction between what are denominated by counsel state buildings, such as the buildings of the State University, or the Capitol, and our school buildings. True, the control of the university is placed in the hands of a board of regents whose duties and powers are perhaps defined with more particularity and detail than are the powers of the boards of education. That may perhaps also be true respecting the State Capitol. Be that as it may, however, the public school buildings and their control are of as much concern to the state as are the other buildings. . . . If it be conceded, therefore, as it is and must be, that the state has not surrendered the control over its buildings to the cities, then it necessarily follows that the terms "public buildings" and "all buildings" used in the [statute] . . . do not embrace all buildings within the cities. Moreover, if state buildings must be excluded, then public school buildings must likewise be excluded from those terms.

Guides for Class Discussion

1. What basic line of reasoning did the court follow in arriving at its decision?

2. Compare this case with *Community Fire District of St. Louis County v. Board of Education, infra.*

3. In your opinion is the law, as propounded by the court in this case, equitable and fair? Give reasons.

4. *"Cities and towns, unless authorized by statute, may not expend municipal funds for the construction of school buildings"* (p. 3).

NELSON V. MAYOR ETC. OF TOWN OF HOMER,
48 La. Ann. 258, 19 So. 271 (1896)
(Decided by the Supreme Court of Louisiana)

[When the Town of Homer attempted to appropriate funds for the support and maintenance of a school, its actions were questioned in court. In arriving at its decision, the court ruled that the municipality, without express permission so to do, may not spend its funds for educational purposes.]

McENERY, J.

The plaintiffs, who are taxpayers in the town of Homer, bring this suit to annul certain ordinances of the corporation establishing a high school, and the ordinances assessing and appropriating five mills of the taxes of 1895 for the support and maintenance of the school. The reason for the nullity of the ordinance is that the corporation of the town of Homer was without power and authority to enact said ordinances, to levy said amount, and appropriate the same for educational purposes. The defense is that under article 209 of the constitution municipal corporations have the power and authority to levy and collect taxes to the amount of 10 mills for municipal purposes, and that an assessment for educational purposes is a municipal regulation. It is further alleged that the corporation, in accordance with Act. No. 110 of 1880, amended its charter, and incorporated this power in it. Under the general welfare clause of the charter, as originally granted, the district judge rendered a judgment in favor of defendants, maintaining the legality of the ordinances and the assessment and appropriation of the tax. The plaintiffs appealed.

. . . Corporations are the creatures of legislative will, and can do no act not authorized by their charters, unless it is by implication necessary to carry out conferred powers. In the original charter there was no grant of any right to the corporation of Homer to erect a school building and maintain a high school. It cannot, by its own act, usurp powers not granted. There was no authority under the act for the corporation to so amend its charter as to authorize the levying of a tax for the maintaining of a high school, or for any other educational purpose. . . . A high school is not essential to municipal government. A system of education is not a part of municipal regulation, and the power of the corporation to establish a public school cannot be inferred from any power necessary for municipal existence. The judgment appealed from is annulled, avoided, and reversed, and it is now ordered that there be judgment for plaintiffs decreeing the nullity of the ordinances mentioned in the petition, and on which the taxing power and assessment is exercised for the levying of the five-mill tax complained of.

Guides for Class Discussion

1. On what basis did the court arrive at its decision?
2. Was the court's reasoning sound?
3. What are the educational implications of this case?

5. *"Municipal officers have no inherent authority to control or manage school property" (p. 3).*

State v. Zeidler,
268 Wis. 34, 66 N.W. (2d) 652 (1954)
(Decided by the Supreme Court of Wisconsin)

[In Milwaukee, Wisconsin, the Board of School Directors, an independent public body, was, by statute, charged with the function of purchasing sites and erecting school buildings. "The schoolhouses and the sites on which they are situated . . . [were] the property of the city," and deeds were made to the city. In 1946 the school district purchased a piece of property to be used as a site for a new building. In 1954, the board not having erected the building, the Common Council of the City of Milwaukee declared the property was no longer needed for public purposes and ordered the proper city officers to sell and convey the property. When the

Mayor and City Clerk refused to execute and sign the deed, on the ground the school directors and not the city council had control of the property and must consent to its conveyance, an action in mandamus was brought to compel them to do so. The trial court issued the writ of mandamus, and the defendants appealed.]

Steinle, Justice.

. . . .

Under the statutes the Board alone is vested with authority to acquire real estate for school purposes. The Common Council has been granted no power in such respect. However, when property is acquired for such purpose, the title is not taken in the name of the Board, but in that of the city. When acquired, the Board utilizes, manages, and controls the property. Jurisdiction to function in such regard has not been granted to the Common Council. . . .

. . . .

The respondents contend that the signing and delivery of the deed by the Mayor and City Clerk constitute ministerial action, the performance of which they may not refuse. It is further contended that it was not within the province of these city officers to "pass upon" the validity of the Common Council resolution. . . .

. . . .

It is especially noted that in his official capacity the Mayor is charged with the responsibility of "taking care that the laws of the state are duly observed and enforced." Were he to knowingly fail in such regard, his conduct might well be construed as nonfeasance in office.

As hereinbefore declared, the Common Council of the city of Milwaukee is not empowered by law to validly direct the conveyance of real estate in control of the Board of School Directors without that body's consent. Were the Mayor to sign the deed, he too would participate in the illegal action of the Common Council and violate the law, the observance of which he is specifically charged to "take care of." . . . It is clear that when the Common Council of the city of Milwaukee by resolution acts legally and within the four corners of its authority in directing a conveyance of property by the Mayor—whether the Mayor signs the resolution, or fails to return it in five days thereby effectuating its passage, or whether it is passed over his veto—then the Mayor thereafter is not in a position to exercise further discretion and decline to sign or deliver the deed. We note that in all of the cases which have come to our attention wherein a Mayor has been compelled by *mandamus* to perform a duty in nature of a ministerial act, the compulsion is based upon mandate of *valid* authority to direct such act. . . .

It seems to us that when it appears that an ordinance or resolution is *invalid*, a Mayor charged with the responsibility of "taking care" that the laws of the state are duly observed and enforced, and that the officers of the city properly discharge their duties, is not to be compelled by *mandamus* to execute a contract provided by an *invalid* ordinance or resolution. Consequently, we conclude that the remedy of *mandamus* does not lie to compel the Mayor of the city of Milwaukee to sign and deliver the deed in question. . . .

Guides for Class Discussion

1. Do you agree with the court in this case? Give reasons.
2. Would a statute authorizing the city council to take the action it did be held constitutional? Why or why not?

6. "*. . . education is a state and not a local affair*" (p. 3).

STATE EX REL. CLARK v. HAWORTH,
122 Ind. 462, 23 N.E. 946 (1890)
(Decided by the Supreme Court of Indiana)

[This was an action against a school trustee to compel him to obey a uniform text book law. He based his refusal to comply with the statute on the ground that it was unconstitutional because it was in violation of the right of local self-government. The lower court held in his favor, but, on appeal, the lower court was reversed, and the act was declared constitutional.]

ELLIOTT, J. . . .

The act assailed does not impinge in the slightest degree upon the right of local self-government. The right of local self-government is an inherent, and not a derivative, one. Individualized, it is the right which a man possesses in virtue of his character as a free man. It is not bestowed by legislatures, nor derived from statutes. But the courts which have carried to its utmost extent the doctrine of local self-government have never so much as intimated that it exists as to a matter over which the constitution has given the law-making power supreme control; nor have they gone beyond the line which separates matters of purely local concern from those of state control. Essentially and intrinsically, *the schools* in which are educated and trained the children who are to become the rulers of the commonwealth *are matters of state, and not of local jurisdiction.* In such matters the state is a unit, and the legislature the source of power. The authority over schools and school affairs is not necessarily a distributive one, to be exercised by local instrumentalities; but, on the contrary, it is a central power, residing in the legislature of the state. It is for the law-making power to determine whether the authority shall be exercised by a state board of education, or distributed to county, township, or city organizations throughout the state. With that determination the judiciary can no more rightfully interfere than can the legislature with a decree or judgment pronounced by a judicial tribunal. The decision is as conclusive and inviolable in the one case as in the other; and an interference with the legislative judgment would be a breach of the constitution which no principle would justify, nor any precedent excuse. [Emphasis supplied.]

Guides for Class Discussion

1. Do you think the courts, today, would accept this decision? Give reasons.
2. What is meant by the "right of local self-government"?
3. Which branch of state government has the authority to determine how the public school system will be organized?
4. What is the real significance of this case?

7. *"A number of courts have held that school property is state property, subject to the exercise of the police power of the state residing in its local school boards; and the municipal authorities may not, therefore, require local school boards to obey their building ordinances or codes"* (p. 3).

City of Bloomfield v. Davis County Community School District,
119 N.W. (2d) 909 (Iowa) (1963)
(Decided by the Supreme Court of Iowa)

[The facts of the case will be found in the material quoted.]

Garfield, Chief Justice.

This is an action in equity by the City of Bloomfield to enjoin defendants, Davis County Community School District, and its contractor, Boatman, from installing in a restricted residence district in plaintiff city a bulk storage tank for gasoline and a pump to supply its school buses therewith. . . . By cross-petition defendants sought to enjoin the city from interfering with their construction of the "facility" and, if a permit therefor is necessary, to compel its issuance by mandamus. Following trial to the court there was a decree for plaintiff from which defendants appeal.

On September 19, 1933, the council of plaintiff city passed ordinance 84 designating and establishing a restricted residence district in the city. Section 2 of the ordinance provides: "That no buildings or other structures, except residences, school houses, churches, and other similar structures shall hereafter be erected, reconstructed, altered, repaired or occupied within said district without first securing from the city council permit therefor . . . ."

. . . .

The only contention of defendants we find it necessary to consider is that ordinance 84 should not be held applicable to them to prevent installation on this school-owned site of this gasoline facility for servicing its school buses because the school district is an arm of the state and proposes to use its property for a governmental purpose.

The ordinance was obviously enacted under the authority of what are now sections 415.1-3, Codes 1958, 1962, I. C. A. and is an exercise of the police power delegated to the city. . . .

The law seems quite well settled that a municipal zoning ordinance is not applicable to the state or any of its agencies in the use of its property for a governmental purpose unless the legislature has clearly manifested a contrary intent. . . .

. . . .

The underlying logic of some . . . authorities is, in substance, that the legislature could not have intended, in the absence of clear expression to the contrary, to give municipalities authority to thwart the state, or any of its agencies in performing a duty imposed upon it by statute.

There can be no doubt the school district is an arm or agency of the state and that the maintenance of public schools, including providing transportation to the pupils entitled to it as required by statute is a governmental function. . . .

. . . .

We think furnishing economical transportation to pupils entitled to it is as much a school matter, over which the district has exclusive jurisdiction, as maintenance of the school buildings or location of the high school football field. (Plaintiff concedes a football stadium is generally held to come within the meaning of a schoolhouse. See also Livingston v. Davis, 243 Iowa 21, 27, 50 N.W. 2d 592, 27 A. L. R. 2d 1237.)

The evidence is undisputed it is economical for the school district to own its buses. It can save eight to ten cents a gallon from buying gasoline for them in bulk and putting it in the buses itself. Bloomfield is maintenance headquarters for the buses the district owns. Many of them have been parked over night for a year or more on the tract where it is proposed to locate this tank and pump. As stated, the district owns the ground. It is most convenient to the school and can be supervised with the same personnel. The school board carefully considered the matter of installing the facility on this site. The state department of public instruction recommended the action the board took. The state fire marshall approved the plans prepared by the architect. No abuse of discretion on the part of anyone is claimed or shown.

Guides for Class Discussion

1. Compare the decision in this case with the one in *State* v. *Zeidler, supra.*
2. Compare the decision in this case with the one in *Community Fire Protection District St. Louis County* v. *Board of Education, infra.*
3. Do you think that this represents "good law"? Give reasons.
4. Under what conditions might a city require a school district to obey a municipal building ordinance?

8. "*. . . in some cases the courts have held that the police power of the municipality takes precedence over the police power of the school board where safety and sanitation are concerned*" (p. 3).

COMMUNITY FIRE PROTECTION DISTRICT OF ST. LOUIS COUNTY v. BOARD OF EDUCATION,
315 S.W. (2d) 873 (Mo.) (1958)
(Decided by the St. Louis Court of Appeals)

[The Missouri courts have consistently refused to follow the general rule that, in the absence of statute to the contrary, other municipalities may not exercise police power over school buildings.

In this case it was held that the police power of a fire district—a municipal corporation—takes precedence over that of the school board.]

JAMES D. CLEMENS, Special Judge.

. . . .

The issue prescribed for us . . . is whether it is the Fire District or the School District to whom the Legislature has granted authority to determine minimum standards for fire protection in the construction of . . . [a] school building.

. . . .

This precise conflict of authority between a statutory fire district and a reorganized school district, has not yet been resolved by our courts. However, our courts have previously dealt with the principle of conflicting authority of public corporations. . . .

Thus, the case of Kansas City v. School District of Kansas City, 356 Mo. 364, 201 S.W. 2d 930, 932, involved the right of the city to exact fees from the school district for inspecting furnace boilers located in the schools. That right depended upon whether the State has reposed in the City or in the school district, "the power and the responsibility of taking measures to protect the people and the property of the people of Kansas City from conflagrations, explosions, smoke nuisances, noxious gases, and casualties which might be caused or occasioned by the facilities of the public school buildings." The Supreme Court analyzed the status of each party and ruled that the school district was not a municipal corporation with diversified powers, but a quasi-public corporation, "the arm and instrumentality of the state for one single and noble purpose, viz., to educate the children of the district." By contrast, the city was held to be possessed of police power, charged with maintaining the safety, health and general welfare of its populace—to be "a miniature state" within its authorized sphere of action. The court then ruled in favor of the city, saying:

"Since the State itself has taken no precautionary measures, and City has been vested with the regulatory and supervisory responsibilities of the exercise of the police power, and School District (having no police power) has not been expressly and specifically given full duty to attend to these responsibilities, we think the Legislature is content in the thought the measures to be taken are within the police power vested in City. . . ."

In the case of Smith v. Board of Education of City of St. Louis, 359 Mo. 264, 221 S.W. 2d 203, 205, the issue was the conflict of powers between the city and the board to regulate school restaurants. By ordinance the city provided for inspection and regulation of all restaurants as to food, utensils, waste disposal and the health and cleanliness of food handlers. By statute, all schools were empowered to operate restaurants, and the commissioner of school buildings in St. Louis was charged with the care of school buildings and was responsible for the sanitary condition thereof. The Supreme Court did not make a specific distinction between the city's possession of police power and the school board's lack thereof, but ruled the conflict in favor of the city as to regulation of the school restaurants because the Legislature had not "expressly and specifically" given the school board "full duty to attend to these responsibilities."

. . . .

. . . Applying here the principles settled in those . . . cases, it is clear to us that the Legislature has subjugated the School District's general power to construct buildings to the Fire District's specific power to regulate the construction of buildings in the furtherance of fire prevention. This is so because of the comparative status of the parties, the Fire District being a municipal corporation endowed with police powers in the field of fire prevention, and the School District being a quasi-public corporation without police power with only the limited power of public education. Inasmuch as the Fire District is exercising police power delegated to it by the State, the School District is just as subservient thereto as if the provisions of the Fire District's ordinances had been prescribed by the State itself. Also, we note that the language granting powers to the School District as to school buildings is directive and elastic, and it is certainly no mandate to erect school buildings in disregard of reasonable building regulations, which the Fire District has been empowered to ordain. So, this result must also prevail because the Legislature, by granting specific power to the Fire District to ordain fire prevention measures is deemed to have denied contrary power to the School District.

. . . .

The respondent School District . . . relies heavily on the case of Salt Lake City v. Board of Education, 52 Utah 540, 175 P. 654. The issue there was quite similar to the case at bar and the city was denied the right to enforce its building restrictions upon the school board. Suffice to say that our Supreme Court has denounced the principle set forth in this Utah case, and said in Kansas City v. School District of Kansas City, supra [356 Mo. 364, 201 S.W. 2d 935]: "We are not disposed to here further analyze these opinions so ably reasoned and written; however, the tendency of decision in harmony with ours herein seems to us more likely to promote the public safety, health and welfare."

. . . .

We conclude that as between these parties, the Legislature has granted to the Fire District the authority to determine the minimum standards for fire prevention and fire protection in the construction of the school building.

Guides for Class Discussion

1. What was the reasoning of the court?
2. Compare this decision with the one in *Salt Lake City* v. *Board of Education of Salt Lake City, supra.* Which represents the "better" law? Give reasons.

9. "*State legislatures may authorize school boards to permit the use of school property for any purpose not prohibited by the constitution, and in a number of states the courts have sustained statutes authorizing a wide use of school buildings*" (p. 3).

Nichols v. School Directors,
93 Ill. 61 (1879)
(Decided by the Supreme Court of Illinois)

[The facts at issue will be found in the quoted material which follows.]

Mr. Justice Sheldon delivered the opinion of the Court:

This was a bill for an injunction by complainant as a citizen, taxpayer and freeholder of the school district of which defendants were directors, to restrain them from allowing the school house of that district to be used by any society or organization for the purpose of a religious meeting house.

The grievance as set forth in the bill is, that the defendants have, as such directors, given permission to different church organizations to hold religious services in the school house, against the protest of complainant and other tax-payers of the district; that under this permission some of the church organizations purpose holding stated meetings in the school house; that by this means complainant is compelled to aid in furnishing a house of worship, and for religious meetings, contrary to the law of the land; that he is opposed to such use of the house by the societies, and that such meetings are about to be held in the same contrary to his wishes, wherefore he prays the injunction.

A demurrer was filed to the bill, which the circuit court sustained, and dissolved the temporary injunction which had been granted, and dismissed the bill. The complainant appealed to this court.

By statute, the supervision and control of school houses is vested in the school directors of the district, and "who may grant the temporary use of school houses, when not occupied by schools, for religious meetings and Sunday schools, for evening schools and for literary societies, and for such other meetings as the directors may deem proper." Rev. Stat. 1874, p. 958, § 39.

There is clearly sufficient warrant in the statute, if that be valid, for the action of the school directors.

But the statute is assailed as being unconstitutional.

The clauses of the constitution which are pointed out as being supposed to be violated by this statute are the following only:

"No person shall be required to attend or support any ministry or place of worship against his consent, nor shall any preference be given by law to any religious denomination or mode of worship." Art. 2, #3.

Art. 8, #3, forbidding, among other public bodies, the General Assembly or any school district from ever making any appropriation or paying from any public fund whatever anything in aid of any church or sectarian purpose, etc.; and forbidding the State or any public corporation from making any grant or donation of land, money or other personal property to any church or for any sectarian purpose.

. . . .

Religion and religious worship are not so placed under the ban of the constitution that they may not be allowed to become the recipient of any incidental benefit whatsoever from the public bodies or authorities of the State. That instrument itself contains a provision authorizing the legislature to exempt property used for religious purposes from taxation; and thereby, the same as is complained of here, there might be indirectly imposed upon the tax-payer the burden of increased taxation, and in that manner the indirect supporting of places of worship. In the respect of the possibility of enhanced taxation therefrom, this provision of the constitution itself is even more obnoxious to objection than this permission given by the school directors to hold religious meetings in the school house. There is no pretence that it is in any way in interference with the occupation of the building for school purposes.

We think the court rightly sustained the demurrer and dismissed the bill, as making no case for an injunction.

The decree will be affirmed.

Decree affirmed.

Guides for Class Discussion

1. Do you think the court today would hold as did the court in this case? Give reasons.

2. Are you in agreement with this decision? Give reasons.

10. *"Some [courts] have permitted the use of schoolhouses for religious meetings of one kind or another provided there was no interference with the regular work of the school" (pp. 3-4).*

SOUTHSIDE ESTATES BAPTIST CHURCH v. BOARD OF TRUSTEES,
115 So. (2d) 697 (Fla.) (1959)
(Decided by the Supreme Court of Florida)

[The facts of this case will be found in the material quoted.]

THORNAL, Justice.

Appellants, who were plaintiffs below, seek reversal of a final decree dismissing their bill of complaint by which they sought an injunction against the temporary use of a public school building for religious meetings.

We must determine whether a Florida public school can be used temporarily as a place of worship during non-school hours.

The appellee, Board of Trustees, permitted several churches to use various school buildings during Sunday non-school hours. The authorization was for the temporary use of the buildings pending completion of construction of church buildings. The record does not show whether the religious groups paid rent nor does it reflect any direct expense to the school trustees. It is clear that the use of the buildings did not interfere with the operation of the school system. The public school system was not in any fashion employed as a medium for the promotion of any religion. The appellants as plaintiffs, sought to enjoin the use of the school buildings for religious purposes. The Chancellor granted a motion to dismiss the amended complaint with prejudice. Reversal of this decree is now sought.

. . . .

While admittedly, there are some differences of view regarding the matter of religious meetings in school houses during non-school periods, we think that logic, as well as our traditional attitudes toward the importance of religious worship, justifies our alignment with those courts which permit such use. . . .

We ourselves have heretofore taken the position that an incidental benefit to a religious group resulting from an appropriate use of public property is not violative of Section 6, of the Declaration of Rights of the Florida Constitution. . . .

In the instant case the Legislature has endowed the trustees of the school district with a reasonable discretion to permit the use of school property during non-school hours "for any legal assembly." We think that the religious observances described in the complaint are well within the category of "legal assembly." . . .

We, therefore, hold that a Board of Trustees of a Florida School District has the power to exercise a reasonable discretion to permit the use of school buildings during non-school hours for any legal assembly which includes religious meetings, subject, of course, to judicial review should such discretion be abused to the point that it could be construed as a contribution of public funds in aid of a particular religious group or as the promotion or establishment of a particular religion.

We think that what we have said disposes also of the contention that the conduct of the appellee trustees is violative of the First Amendment to the Constitution of the United States, which provides in part that, "Congress shall make no law respecting an establishment of religion, or prohibiting the free exercise thereof; . . ." as the same has been made applicable to the states under the due process provision of the Fourteenth Amendment. We find nothing in the conduct of the appellee trustees to suggest the involvement of public funds or property in the establishment of a religion or in preferring one religious faith over another. We agree with those courts which have observed that in the ultimate the American people are basically religious. Their spiritual or theological views might differ, but by and large, they are committed to the ideal that there should be a place for any and all religions in the scheme of our community and social life.

The Chancellor ruled correctly in dismissing the amended complaint with prejudice. His decree is, therefore, affirmed.

Guides for Class Discussion

1. Compare this case with *Spencer* v. *Joint School District, infra.*

2. Are you in agreement with the court's thinking in this case? Give reasons.

3. What are some of the implications which this case has for school administration?

11. *"Some [courts] . . . have held that no kind of religious exercises could be held in a schoolhouse unless specifically authorized by statute" (pp. 3-4).*

SPENCER V. JOINT SCHOOL DISTRICT,
15 Kan. 259 (1875)
(Decided by the Supreme Court of Kansas)

[This was an action brought to restrain the defendant district from leasing its school building for other than school purposes. Primarily, the objection related to the use of the building for religious purposes. The district demurred, and the trial court sustained the demurrer. On appeal, this decision of the trial court was overthrown.]

BREWER, J.: . . . .

. . . .

. . . . the question as it comes before us, may fairly be thus stated: May the majority of the taxpayers and electors in a school-district, for other than school purposes use or permit the use of the school-house built with funds raised by taxation? The question is one which in view of the times, and the attacks made in so many places, and from so many directions, upon our public-school system, justifies, as it has received at our hands, most serious consideration. We are fully aware of the fact, that all over the state the school-house is, by general consent, or at least without active opposition, used for a variety of purposes other than the holding of public schools. Sabbath schools of separate religious denominations, church assemblies, sometimes political meetings, social gatherings, etc., are held there. Now none of these can be strictly considered among the purposes for which a public building can be erected, or taxation employed. But it often happens, particularly in our newer settlements, that there is no other public building than the school-house—no place so convenient as that. The use for these purposes works little damage. It is used by the inhabitants of the district whose money has built it, and used for their profit or pleasure. Shall it be said that this is illegal? . . . The public school-house cannot be used for any private purposes. The argument is a short one. Taxation is invoked to raise funds to erect the building; but taxation is illegitimate to provide for any private purpose. Taxation will not lie to raise funds to build a place for a religious society, a political society, or a social club. What cannot be done directly, cannot be done indirectly. As you may not levy taxes to build a church, no more may you levy taxes to build a school-house and then lease it for a church.

Nor is it an answer to say that its use for school purposes is not interfered with, and that the use for the other purposes works little, perhaps no immediately-perceptible injury to the building, and results in the receipt of immediate pecuniary benefit. . . . The use of a public school-house for a single religious or political gathering, is, legally, as unauthorized as its constant use therefor. True, a court of equity would not interfere by injunction after a single use, and where there was no likelihood of a repetition of the wrong, for it is only apprehended wrongs that equity will enjoin. Here the unauthorized use is charged as a frequent fact, and one likely to occur hereafter. It is unnecessary to pursue this discussion further, for it would be simply traveling over a road already well worn and dusty. . . .

The judgment of the district court will be reversed, and the case remanded for further proceedings in accordance with the views herein expressed.

Guides for Class Discussion

1. Trace the line of reasoning followed by the court.
2. Compare this decision with the one rendered by the court in *Southside Estates Baptist Church* v. *Board of Trustees, supra.*

12. "The courts . . . have approved the leasing of school property for the drilling of oil and gas, although the opposite has also been held" (p. 4).

WILLIAMS v. McKENZIE,
203 Ky. 376, 262 S.W. 598 (1924)
(Decided by the Court of Appeals of Kentucky)

[In Kentucky, where the statute gave a county board of education the authority to hold and dispose of school property for the use and benefit of the district, its authority to execute a lease for the drilling of oil on school lands was questioned. The lower court held that the board did not have the authority in question and, on appeal, the higher court reversed its decision.]

Turner, C. . . .

. . . .

But it is earnestly argued that, the county board of education being the creature of the statute for a specific purpose, its only duty and authority lies in the administration of educational affairs; that it is not authorized to go into the field of speculation and engage in hazardous industrial affairs, even though such activities might result profitably, and for that reason alone the oil lease given by the school board was invalid and properly cancelled. . . .

In support of this argument reliance is had upon the case of Herald v. Board of Education, 65 W. Va. 765, 65 S.E. 102, 31 L. R. A. (N. S.) 588. In that case it was held by a majority of the Supreme Court of West Virginia that a school board under the statutes of that state had no power to lease a schoolhouse lot for oil and gas purposes, even though the school authorities had the absolute fee-simple title thereto.

. . . .

Oil and gas are fugitive minerals; they are connected by underground streams or crevices by which they may be drained from one property onto another, and there brought to the surface. There can be no sound or practical reason given that will deprive school authorities who own property under which there are valuable minerals from entering into contracts for its development, and particularly would this seem to be true when the character of the mineral is such that adjoining landowners may profit at the expense of the school property by the failure of the school authorities to enter such contracts. . . . There was, however, in the West Virginia case referred to, a strong dissenting opinion, in which we fully concur. That opinion, after discussing the West Virginia statute, said:

"I think the statute not only expressly but impliedly gives this board ample power to lease this property. This ought especially to be so where the product, as in this case, is oil and gas, fugitive in nature and which will be drained and carried away by operations on adjoining lands."

We are of the opinion, therefore, that under the statute in existence at the time the title was conveyed to the school authorities the board of education had the right to execute the lease in question, and, having the right to do so, it was its duty to do so to prevent the valuable mineral product on the school property from being appropriated by others.

Guides for Class Discussion

1. Do you agree with the court, or do you prefer the decision of the West Virginia court in the case cited? Give reasons.

2. Do you agree with the court when it says the board not only
    had the authority or right to take the action it did, but it had
    the duty of so doing? Give reasons.

13. *"As a rule, school boards are vested with specific statutory
authority to acquire school sites, but even in the absence of such
authority the courts hold that authority to build school buildings
carries with it, by necessary implication, authority to purchase
school sites"* (p. 4).

STATE v. BOARD OF EDUCATION,
71 W. Va. 52, 76 S.E. 127 (1912)

(Decided by the Supreme Court of Appeals of West Virginia)

[Pertinent facts will be found in the following quotation.]

BRANNON, P.

The school district of Clarksburg by vote authorized the incurrence
of a debt and the issue of bonds for its payment for the purpose of building
one high school and two graded schools. The bonds were sold, and their
proceeds are in the treasury. The board of education refused to build
the high school and one graded school out of such money, on the ground
that to do so would call for the purchase of ground for their erection,
and the board doubted its power to use any of the money coming from
said bonds in acquiring such ground. Howard Post asks of this court a
mandamus to compel the board to build said high school and graded
school, and to acquire sites for them, and use such bond money in
doing so.

Act 1908, c. 27, § 13 (Code Supp. 1909, c. 45, § 1571), says that the
board of education of every district shall provide by purchase or condemnation "suitable schoolhouses and grounds." Act 1911, c. 70, allows the board
to "borrow money and issue bonds for the purpose of building, completing,
enlarging, repairing or furnishing schoolhouses." . . . When the statute says
that the money may be used to build houses, it means that it may be used
to acquire land for schoolhouses. Necessarily so. It is a necessary implication, if the words do not per se mean land, as here used. Commanded to
build schoolhouses, it is an incidental power because indispensable to

attain the end. You cannot build a schoolhouse without land on which to build it.

In view of the law above stated, and in view of the purpose which must have been in the minds of the legislators who enacted the bond section, we hold that the word "schoolhouses" includes land for schoolhouses. We hold that the section in giving the board of education power to apply the money arising from the bonds "for the purpose of building, completing, enlarging, repairing or furnishing schoolhouses" meant to give the board power to acquire land on which to build schoolhouses. We can see that the Legislature never designed to limit the use of the money to work and material of construction, and deny its use in acquiring the ground indispensable and preliminary to work of construction. This ground is the first thing requisite in carrying out the purpose of the statute —a sine qua non. Otherwise the statute might be abortive. . . . Think of the intent and purpose, as we must do when construing a statute. Think of the evil to be remedied, the object to be accomplished, and give such a statute such a construction as will effectuate its purpose. We think the other construction would be cramped and technical, forgetful of the spirit, sticking to the mere letter.

Guides for Class Discussion

1. Compare this case with *Reiger v. Board of Education, infra.*
2. Do you agree with the court's decision? Give reasons.

14. "Authority to purchase school sites carries with it by implication authority to purchase the necessary playgrounds and athletic fields, and these do not have to be adjacent to the lot on which the schoolhouse is situated" (p. 4).

REIGER v. BOARD OF EDUCATION,
287 Ill. 590, 122 N.E. 838 (1919)
(Decided by the Supreme Court of Illinois)

[The board of education of Springfield, Illinois, purchased certain real estate, which was a block and a half from the nearest schoolhouse and was not acquired as a schoolhouse site. When it began to erect improvements necessary to the conversion of the property into recreational grounds and athletic fields, this action was brought to restrain the board from completing the payment for the property. Plaintiffs did not deny that playgrounds and athletic fields were "necessary grounds" within the meaning of a statute authorizing the board " 'to buy or lease sites for schoolhouses with the necessary grounds' etc.," but they contended that such power could only be exercised "in connection with the buying or leasing of 'sites for schoolhouses' and that the 'necessary grounds' must be connected with and a part of the school site and actually contiguous to the same." The lower court ruled in favor of the board, and the court, here, upheld its decision.]

DUNCAN, C. J. . . .

       .   .   .   .

. . . We cannot agree that a reasonable construction of clause 5 of section 127 requires that necessary school grounds shall be purchased in connection with the purchase of a school site or that such necessary grounds must be contiguous to a schoolhouse site already purchased. It is very easy to conceive of a situation where it would not be possible to acquire additional necessary school grounds contiguous to a site already purchased by reason of the surrounding property being held by other property owners and not obtainable at a reasonable figure. Said clause 5 empowers the board to buy or lease sites for schoolhouses, with the necessary school grounds, and it contains no requirement that the necessary school grounds must all be contiguous to the schoolhouse site. We are therefore not authorized to give it such an interpretation, particularly in cases where it might be shown that it is not possible to purchase other suitable grounds contiguous to one or more sites already purchased. The statute necessarily gives a board of education large discretion in the selection of school grounds, and where there are a number of schools in a school district it is clearly evident that grounds not connected with any of the school sites might be used as playgrounds for the pupils of a number of schools, and would serve the necessity of such schools equally as well, or better, than if contiguous to any one site and at very much less cost.

Guides for Class Discussion

1. Do you think the court would have held as it did had the facts indicated that the property in question was to be used for the benefit of the pupils enrolled in a single school?

2. Would the court have held as it did if there had been no statute authorizing a school board to obtain sites and construct buildings? Give reasons for your answer.

15. *"School boards are vested with authority to accept donations of property to be used for school purposes, but when school boards accept such a donation they will be required to administer it perpetually according to the terms of the donor"* (p. 4).

MAXCY v. CITY OF OSHKOSH,
144 Wis. 238, 128 N.W. 899 (1910)
(Decided by the Supreme Court of Wisconsin)

[A grant was made to the City of Oshkosh, Wisconsin, for the purpose of constructing a manual training school, contingent upon the city raising and providing an additional $50,000. When the common council passed a resolution accepting the gift and providing for the issuance and sale of bonds in the amount of $50,000 to meet its obligation, an action was brought to restrain the city from using the proceeds of the bond sale for this purpose. The court, here, commented at some length on the responsibility of the municipality in case it accepted the donation.]

BARNES, J. . . .

. . . .

It is further urged that, a trust in perpetuity being created by the will, the property devoted to the charitable use must always be applied to such use, and that it is beyond the power of the city of Oshkosh to raise money to build a manual training school which must be forever maintained as such. This contention raises one of the most difficult questions in the case. The general rule of law is that money or property devoted to a charitable use where a trust is created must, if the gift is accepted, be irrevocably devoted to such use, and that in case of attempted diversion a court of equity will intervene, and if necessary name a new trustee to carry out the objects and purposes of the trust. In other words, the term "perpetuity" as applied to charitable trusts has retained its original significance, in that it means an inalienable and indestructible interest. Generally speaking, any limitation that suspends the power of alienation beyond the period allowed by law creates a perpetuity; but we are not dealing with a perpetuity of this kind.

However, this general language in reference to the meaning of a perpetuity as applied to a charitable trust cannot be taken too literally. . . . No one is wise enough to say what social changes the mutations of time may bring about or what political or other cataclysms the future may witness. . . . We must presume that the city of Oshkosh will live and thrive, and that the system of free district schools guaranteed by the Constitution will be maintained therein. We must also presume that instruction in the languages, in mathematics, and in other subjects now taught therein will be continued. The tendency of the times is to enlarge the school curriculum instead of reducing it. It is fair to assume that any branch of knowledge that has been firmly ingrafted in our system of education has come to stay, and there is nothing in the record to indicate that manual training in our public schools has not come to stay. Of course laws may be passed in the future that will prohibit the teaching of manual training; but the testatrix knew of this possibility when she made her gift and was willing to take the chances. . . . Mrs. Beach knew when she made her will that the school building she was providing for might not, and in fact could not, endure for all time. Fire might destroy it, and, if it did not, time would disintegrate it and render it unfit for use. Conditions might demand that a newer, more commodious and more modern building should be constructed at some time in the future, even before the building provided for had ceased to be serviceable. All the city will have to do to comply with the terms of the will will be to place such a memorial tablet in the new building as was placed in the old, and carry on a system of instruction therein in harmony with the expressed wish of the testatrix. . . . The undertaking of the city of Oshkosh to perpetually maintain this school is not contrary to the letter of the law. . . . When the city of Oshkosh accepted its charter, it subjected itself to the burdens imposed by the Constitution. One of those burdens was the maintenance of a system of district schools in which education should be free to all pupils of school age, so long as the city existed and so long as the provision of the Constitution survived; or, in other words, in perpetuity. . . .

Guides for Class Discussion

1. Do you think the fact that the municipality had been authorized to maintain schools by virtue of its charter affected the thinking of the court? If so, how?

2. Had the grant been made to a school district instead of a city, do you think the court would have ruled as it did? Give reasons.

16. *"School boards, under statutory authority, may take private property by the exercise of the right of eminent domain; and, when they do so, the courts will permit them a wide exercise of discretion both with respect to the need of taking the property and the amount to be taken" (p. 4).*

STATE V. STOJACK,
53 Wash. (2d) 55, 330 P. (2d) 567 (1958)
(Decided by the Supreme Court of Washington)

[A school district, to condemn land contiguous to a 73-acre site which it already owned, brought a condemnation action. The trial court refused to enter a decree of public use and necessity which would have permitted the district to condemn the property. In an original proceeding for a writ of certiorari for a review of the trial court's order, the higher court approved the district's efforts at condemnation.]

WEAVER, Justice.

.   .   .   .

A municipal corporation does not have an inherent power of eminent domain. It may exercise such power only when it is expressly authorized to do so by the state legislature. . . .

Of course, by statute, the state may delegate the power of eminent domain to one of its political subdivisions, but such statutes are strictly construed. . . .

.   .   .   .

The trial court erred when it concluded that the school district was not entitled to condemn defendant's property because the district already owned 73 acres of land.

.   .   .   .

Public education is a public use for which private property may be appropriated under the power of eminent domain. If an attempt is made to take more property than is reasonably necessary to accomplish the purpose, then the taking of excess property is no longer a public use, and a certificate of public use and necessity must be denied.

In the selection of a site, the board of directors had the authority to determine the area of land reasonably necessary to accommodate suitable buildings, play grounds . . ., student activity areas, and related facilities to establish an adequate senior high school in accordance with present day educational requirements. . . .

Generally, the action of a public agency or a municipal corporation having the right of eminent domain in selecting land for a public use will not be controlled by the courts, except for a manifest abuse of discretion, violation of law, fraud, improper motives, or collusion. This court has frequently held that, in eminent domain proceedings, selection of land to be condemned by the proper public agency is conclusive in the absence of bad faith, or arbitrary, capricious, or fraudulent action.

Guides for Class Discussion

1. What, in your mind, is the real significance of this decision?
2. As a result of this decision, what limitations, if any, are placed on the board's authority to take property by eminent domain?

17. *"When property is taken by the right of eminent domain, the courts will require the board to pay the owner a fair market price for the property when put to its most profitable use; the owner of land taken by eminent domain must be compensated for whatever loss he suffers"* (p. 4).

SARGENT v. TOWN OF MERRIMAC,
196 Mass. 171, 81 N.E. 970 (1907)
(Decided by the Supreme Judicial Court of Massachusetts, Essex)

[This was an action against the Town of Merrimac for compensation for land taken by defendant for a water supply. The main question before the court was the value of the land in question for the special purpose to which it could be put. In its decision, the court commented on the need for properly compensating the owner for the property taken.]

LORING, J. This is a petition to obtain compensation for the taking of a lot of land by the defendant town for a water supply. The lot in question contained good water adapted in quantity and quality for the supply of the town. There was evidence that the water in question was the only ground water in the neighborhood fit for the needs of the defendant town, but that there was a lake or pond of water which would be fit in respect of quantity and quality if treated by filtration. The case is here on exceptions taken by the petitioner.

· · · · · · · · · · · · · · · · · · · ·

What the petitioner was entitled to receive was the fair market value of the land of her testator as it was at the time of the taking. Market value in this connection does not mean the same thing that market value means when the market value of flour or other things dealt in daily in the market is spoken of. A lot of land cannot have a market value in that sense of the word. What is meant by the market value of land is the value of the land in the market; that is to say, for the purposes of sale.

The market value to which the petitioner was entitled was made up of the value of the land apart from its special adaptability for water supply purposes, plus such sum as a purchaser would have added to that value because of the chance that the land in question might be some day used as a water supply. Moulton v. Newburyport Water Co., 137 Mass. 163.

Guides for Class Discussion

1. What did the court hold with respect to the determination of the value of property taken? Do you agree?

2. Do you think the rule laid down by the court is applicable to a case where the property is taken by a quasi-municipal corporation such as a school district, rather than by a municipal corporation? Justify your answer.

18. "When land is taken by eminent domain, the fee remains with
the original owner, unless the statutes provide otherwise, and when
the property is no longer used for school purposes it reverts to the
original owner" (p. 4).

MULLIGAN V. SCHOOL DISTRICT,
241 Pa. St. 204, 88 A. 362 (1913)
(Decided by the Supreme Court of Pennsylvania)

[This was an action to recover the money paid to a school district
for property which the district had previously taken as the result
of the exercise of the right of eminent domain. Some years after
taking the property the district abandoned it for school purposes
and sold it to one Morris for $1,000. The officials of the district
executed a deed to Morris purportedly conferring a fee and "con-
taining a convenant of general warranty." Later, the heirs of one
Lazarus who had earlier purchased from the owners of the property
their right, title, and interest in it, brought an action of ejectment
against Morris, to recover the land. This resulted in a judgment in
favor of Lazarus' heirs. Morris subsequently died and his heirs
brought this action against the district to recover the $1,000 which
Morris had paid for the property. The trial court ruled for plaintiff
but its decision was overruled on appeal. At issue was the nature
of the title which the district took following the exercise of the
right of eminent domain.]

MOSCHZISKER, J. . . .

.   .   .   .

The statement of claim shows that the plaintiff's action was expressly
founded upon a breach of the covenant of general warranty contained in
the deed to their decedent. School districts are creatures of the statutes
and only have such powers as are thereby given to them. They are "corporations of lower grade and less power than a city, have less the characteris-
tics of private corporations and more of a mere agent of the state. They are
territorial divisions for the purposes of the common school laws; and their
officers have no power except by express statutory grant and necessary
implication." Erie School District v. Fuess, 98 Pa. 600, 606. No act of
assembly has been cited to us, and we know of none, which either expressly or impliedly grants or attempts to grant the right or confer the
power upon a school district to convey in fee property acquired by it in

the exercise of the power of eminent domain, or in such a case to enter into a covenant of general warranty of title; and in law the plaintiff's decedent must have been aware of this when he accepted the deed and paid the purchase money. Moreover, even though from all the facts in the case the inference might be deduced that a conveyance to the purchaser had been authorized by action of the school board, the plaintiffs were unable to produce the minutes and there were no proofs from which it could justifiably be found that the officials who signed the deed had been formally authorized to bind the district by a covenant of general warranty. The conclusion we are forced to is hard upon the estate of the plaintiff's decedent, but it is clear beyond doubt that the referee and the learned court below erred when they permitted a recovery in this case.

Guides for Class Discussion

1. While the court ruled that the board did not have the right to "convey in fee property acquired by it in the exercise of the power of eminent domain," it ruled against plaintiffs. Why?
2. How do you think the court would have held if, by statute, the board had been authorized to take title in fee simple? Give reasons.

19. *"When property is conveyed to a school board and the deed clearly provides for the reversion of the property to the original owner when no longer used for school purposes, the board does not own the property in fee simple, and it reverts to the original owner or his heirs when no longer used for school purposes"* (pp. 4-5).

Consolidated School District v. Walter,
243 Minn. 159, 66 N.W. (2d) 881 (1954)
(Decided by the Supreme Court of Minnesota)

[This was an action to enjoin defendants from entering upon certain real estate which, in 1863, had been conveyed to a school district for use as a site for a schoolhouse. The original conveyance provided that whenever the tract of land ceased to be used as the site for a schoolhouse it should revert to the owner, " 'his wife, their heirs and assigns.' " Subsequently the executor of the estate of the original owner conveyed the entire tract of land to one Hartley Mars. By other conveyances, the land eventually came into the hands of defendant. None of the deeds to the tract of land made reference to the part conveyed to the district in 1863. Defendant, acting upon the assumption that the district ceased to make use of the property as a public school took possession of the property. Plaintiff district then brought this action to have the ownership of the school site determined. The district court ruled in favor of defendant and the plaintiff appealed. The higher court reversed the lower court, holding that a possibility of reverter was not alienable and defendants, as a result, acquired no interest in the site. It ruled that only the grantor and his heirs could recover the property when it ceased to be used as a school site.]

DELL, Chief Justice.

. . . .

We choose to determine first what interests passed under the Ayres deed made in 1863. Clearly the intent was to create a charitable trust—the Ayres being the settlors; the school district, the trustee; and the inhabitants of the district, the beneficiaries. . . .

. . . .

It appears to us that the intent of the grantor, as expressed in the deed and in light of the surrounding circumstances, was to convey the land to the school district in fee for so long as it was needed for the purpose given. It does not appear tenable to us that he merely intended to give the school district a right of user in the land, retaining ownership in himself. The vast majority of cases involving similar grants of land to school districts have reached the same conclusion.

Whether the qualified fee involved here is a fee determinable by a special limitation, or a fee subject to a condition subsequent, does not materially affect the result in this case. However, the failure to properly distinguish these two types of qualified fees has caused unnecessary confusion and is worthy of brief comment. Theoretically, if the grantor intends to insure compliance with a condition by providing for forfeiture upon breach, a fee upon condition subsequent arises; but if the intent is to give the property as long as it is needed for a specified use and no longer, then a determinable fee is created. The practical distinction between the two rests largely in their manner of termination. Under a condition subsequent, the grantor or his heirs must exercise his right of reentry upon breach of the condition or the estate continues in the grantee. There is no such election by the grantor in a determinable fee. In the latter case, the property reverts back to the grantor or his heirs automatically without any action on his part upon the happening of the special limitation. It is often difficult to ascertain the intent of the grantor, and exhaustive study could, no doubt, uncover factually identical cases with opposite results. The deed in this case does not contain the common indicia for creating a fee subject to a condition subsequent nor does it provide for the right of reentry, although this provision has been held not to be essential. On the other hand the deed does provide that "whenever said School House ceases to be used . . ." the estate will "determine" and "revert." This language, although not technically precise, more closely resembles that used in a conveyance of a determinable fee. Cases with similar facts support this construction. . . .

. . . .

Despite vigorous criticism of the rule, the authorities generally concede that possibilities of reverter were not alienable at common law, and this was apparently assumed to be the law in Minnesota prior to 1937. The reason commonly given for the common-law rule was that possibilities of reverter were too nebulous to be conveyed unless coupled with a reversionary interest. . . .

Guides for Class Discussion

1. Compare this decision with the one in *Washington City Board of Education* v. *Edgerton, infra.*
2. Distinguish between this decision and the one in *Scott County Board of Education* v. *Pepper, infra.*
3. Differentiate between a fee determinable by a special limitation and a fee subject to a condition subsequent.
4. Do you think that the court, in distinguishing between these two types of qualified fees, was guilty of recognizing a "distinction" without a "difference"? Give reasons.

20. ". . . *the courts do not look with favor on deeds that provide for reverter of school property, and such deeds will be construed strictly against the grantor*" (p. 5).

WASHINGTON CITY BOARD OF EDUCATION V. EDGERTON,
244 N.C. 576, 94 S.E. (2d) 661 (1956)
(Decided by the Supreme Court of North Carolina)

[This was an action by a board of education to determine title to a city lot which defendant agreed to purchase from the board. The lower court held the board had the right to convey the property free of any reversionary interest. The higher court upheld this decision. The facts of the case will be found in the material quoted.]

DEVIN, Justice.

In 1808 by an act of the General Assembly of North Carolina, Chapter LXXV, the trustees of the Washington Academy were created a corporate body, and as such acquired fee simple title to the land described in the pleadings, and erected thereon a building which was used thereafter by the trustees for conducting a school. In 1904 successor trustees of the Washington Academy conveyed this property by deed to the Board of School Trustees of the Town of Washington and their successors for a nominal consideration "upon condition that the same shall be held and possessed by the party of the second part only so long as the said property shall be used for school purposes."

Thereafter a 3-story brick school building was erected on the property and continuously used for school purposes until March, 1956, when the building was sold and removed, a new school building having been erected on another site, and the land was offered for sale at public auction in accord with the statute. The defendant Edgerton became the last and highest bidder in the amount of $77,800. It was stipulated that the plaintiff, the Washington City Board of Education, a body corporate, is one and the same as the Board of Trustees of the Washington City Administrative Unit and the Board of School Trustees of the Town of Washington, by virtue of pertinent statutes.

.   .   .   .

After a careful study of all the facts and circumstances in this case in the light of previous decisions of this Court, we reach the conclusion that the language used in the habendum clause in the deed of 1904 was not intended to impose rigid restrictions upon the title or to create a condition subsequent, but that it was intended by the parties thereby to indicate the motive and purpose of the transfer of title. It expresses no power of termination or right of re-entry for condition broken.

"A clause in a deed will not be construed as a condition subsequent, unless it expresses in apt and appropriate language the intention of the parties to this effect . . . and a mere statement of the purpose for which the property is to be used is not sufficient to create such condition." Hall v. Quinn, 190 N.C. 326, 130 S.E. 18, 20; Oxford Orphanage v. Kittrell, 223 N.C. 427, 27 S.E. 2d 133.

. . . .

The law does not favor a construction of the language in a deed which will constitute a condition subsequent unless the intention of the parties to create such a restriction upon the title is clearly manifested. . . . And where the language in the deed merely expresses the motive and purpose which prompted the conveyance, without reservation of power of termination or right of re-entry for condition broken, an unqualified fee will pass.

Guides for Class Discussion

1. Compare this decision with the one rendered in *Scott County Board of Education* v. *Pepper, infra.*
2. On what basis did the court arrive at its decision?

21. "*Where property was deeded to school districts 'for school purposes only,' 'so long as the property shall be used for school purposes and no longer,' or 'to be used for school property in perpetuity,' courts have held that the property did not revert to the grantor when no longer used for school purposes*" (p. 5).

Scott County Board of Education v. Pepper,
311 S.W. (2d) 189 (Ky.) (1958)
(Decided by the Court of Appeals of Kentucky)

[This was an action brought by a board of education to quiet title to a tract of land that had been conveyed to it in 1915 " 'for the purpose of a common school house, and for no other purpose.' " The conveyance was made following the receipt of $225 paid by the board, and the deed was signed by the grantor whose heirs now claimed title to it as reversioners. There appeared to be no reason why the board should deny that it had ceased to use the land for the purpose of a common school, and it had attempted to sell the site for $3,000. The only question was whether the board's interest continued in the property after it ceased to use it or whether it reverted to the grantor's heirs.]

MILLIKEN, Judge.

.　.　.　.　.　.　.　.　.　.　.　.　.　.　.　.　.　.　.

The question is whether the Board obtained a fee simple title by the conveyance or some type of defeasible fee. The criteria applicable here are summarized in the Restatement of the Law of Property, Section 44, note m., pages 129-130:

"When a limitation merely states the purpose for which the land is conveyed, such limitation usually does not indicate an intent to create an estate in fee simple which is to expire automatically upon the cessation of use for the purpose named. Additional facts, however, can cause such an intent to be found. Among the facts sufficient to have this result are clauses in other parts of the same instrument, the relation between the consideration paid for the conveyance and the market value of the land in question, and the situation under which the conveyance was obtained.

"Illustrations:

"18. A, owning Blackacre in fee simple absolute, transfers Blackacre 'to B and his heirs to and for the use of the C Church and for no other purpose.' B has an estate in fee simple absolute and not an estate in fee simple determinable."

The quoted words from the deed to the Board are not the usual words of limitation such as "during," "as long as," "until," and the like which result in creating an estate upon limitation, automatically terminating at the time specified. . . . Nor are they the usual words of condition such as "on condition that," "provided that" or "on these express conditions," which technically require an ejectment or re-entry to cause the title to revert. . . . In fact, it is the general rule that conveyances of land for stated purposes, and for no other, do not create fees upon limitations or express provisions for reverter when such uses cease. . . .

This court has consistently held to the general rule in deeds of this nature and refused to create a right of reversion where none was expressly stated or inescapably implied.

Guides for Class Discussion

1. Do you agree with the reasoning of the court in this case? Give reasons.

2. What does this case add to your knowledge of the subject of "reversion"?

22. *"Before a court will declare a forfeiture, it must be very clear that school authorities intended to abandon the use of property for school purposes" (p. 5).*

Harris v. Consolidated School District,
328 S.W. (2d) 646 (Mo.) (1959)
(Decided by the Supreme Court of Missouri)

[This was an action to quiet title to property conveyed to a school district by a deed which contained a reverter clause. The main issue was whether a school district had abandoned the use of school property so as to make it possible for the title to revert to the heirs of the original grantor, or rather, to one holding a quit-claim deed from the heirs. The trial court ruled that, even though classes ceased to be taught in the school building located on the site in question, and some rooms in the building were used for the storage of miscellaneous materials, and one room was rented for use as a grocery store, the district had not abandoned the property. The higher court upheld the decision of the lower court, in an appeal by plaintiffs.]

Eager, Judge.

. . . .

We have determined that the trial court was correct in holding that no reverter had been shown as of the date of filing suit. The reverter clause, as a whole, must be construed to mean that the property shall revert when, and only when, it is no longer used "for a school site"; the last part of the clause merely says "when they fail and cease *using* it . . ." (without specification of purpose), but we must fairly infer the purpose previously stated. A cessation of use, as so referred to, is not a momentary or casual one; we think that such a clause necessarily implies a thought and intent of permanency in the change. No one could well claim that a cessation of classes for a day, a week, a month, or even for a term, would effect a reverter, if they were to be resumed thereafter. . . . The dominant issue is whether the building has, with a reasonable prospect of permanency, ceased to be a school, in view of its continued use for school storage, and the considered possibility of its future use for classes. . . . We shall not presume to fix any date when abandonment would take place. A school district may not arbitrarily retain title to property under such a conveyance unless it is done in good faith and with some reasonable purpose and intent. We do hold that neither at the filing of the suit nor at the time of the trial had there been a reverter. This, however, is no adjudication for all future times. The use of one room as a grocery concerned the trial court considerably; it held that the evidence was not competent because the pleadings had not been amended to show a reliance thereon as an abandonment. . . . On the merits we do not consider the temporary use of one room of the building as a grocery store as in any way controlling. It is apparent that the district was thereby able to effect some repairs to the building, without expending public money; the occupancy could be terminated promptly on notice. We all know that ordinarily a building is better preserved when occupied than when vacant. Actually, the parties simply agreed to mitigate the loss and damage from deterioration. We hold that such temporary occupancy did not affect the status. If more were needed, we might look to the admitted oral agreement that this occupancy should not affect the present litigation; presumably, that bound the parties plaintiff and defendant. We may note here that plaintiff, in adopting this theory of the materiality and competency of subsequent events (and plaintiff still urges the point here), is also precluded from objecting to our consideration of such expressed discussions and intentions of the board as may have occurred after suit was file [*sic*]. We, therefore, hold that as of the date of the judgment there had been no abandonment or reverter.

Guides for Class Discussion

1. Distinguish between this case and the three that precede it.
2. Do you agree with the court's thinking? Give reasons.

23. *"In the exercise of its discretion to select school sites, a school board will not have its discretion controlled by the courts so long as it is exercised in good faith and not abused" (p. 5).*

PIKE COUNTY BOARD OF EDUCATION V. FORD,
279 S.W. (2d) 245 (Ky.) (1955)
(Decided by the Court of Appeals of Kentucky)

[When the plaintiff school board attempted to obtain certain land for a site for a schoolhouse it could not agree with the owner concerning the price, and it brought a condemnation proceedings. The trial court set the price at $12,000 and awarded damages in the amount of $1,000, and an appeal was taken to the circuit court, which found the value of the land to be $15,350 and made no award for damages. This appeal was from that judgment. In arriving at its decision, here, the court found it necessary to comment on the authority of a board to condemn property.]

CAMMACK, Judge.

.   .   .   .

A school board is vested with the authority to select public school sites, subject only to the limitation that it cannot act arbitrarily or beyond the pale of sound discretion. . . . In the case of Perry County Board of Education v. Deaton, 311 Ky. 227, 223 S.W. 2d 882, 883, we said:

"County Boards of Education are given broad discretion under KRS 160.160 and 160.290 in the selection of school sites and in the establishment of schools as they deem necessary for the promotion of education and the general welfare of the pupils. As stated in Phelps v. Witt, 304 Ky. 473, 201 S.W. 2d 4, and Justice v. Clemons, 308 Ky. 820, 215 S.W. 2d 992, when the Board has obtained the approval of the Superintendent of Public Instruction of its plans for a new building (KRS 162.060) courts will not interfere with the proposed plans unless there is positive proof of fraud, collusion or a clear abuse of discretion. The obligation of locating school sites rests with the County Board of Education. It is not for the courts to say whether the Board has acted wisely or unwisely in determining where the school should be located. The only question for the courts' determination is whether the Board is exceeding its authority or is acting arbitrarily."

The testimony of Paul W. Thurman, Director of School Building Grounds for the State Department of Education, shows that the superintendent of Public Instruction was consulted about the proposed site and that the location was approved by the Department. There is no evidence showing fraud, collusion or abuse of discretion on the part of the School Board. Consequently, the court exceeded its authority when, on its own motion, it undertook to question the wisdom of choosing this particular site for the school. . . .

We think also that the court erred in holding that the Board was without authority to condemn the land under lease to the Columbian Fuel Corporation. An authority with the power to condemn is not limited to its immediate needs only, but it may, and indeed should, give consideration to future needs. . . .

.   .   .   .

The fact that a portion of the land taken will continue to be put to private use by a public utility, holding a lease thereon until the needs of the Board require its use, does not destroy the right of eminent domain. The Board had authority to take whatever interest the appellees had in the property and to leave for future negotiation the question of the corporation's interest. . . .

Guides for Class Discussion

1. Do you think it proper that the court should not interfere with a school board in the selection of a school site in the absence of evidence that the board abused its discretion or acted arbitrarily? Justify your answer.
2. Compare this case with *Sarratt* v. *Cash, infra.*

24. *"A school board must be free to exercise its discretion . . . at the time it makes the determination of a school site; it cannot limit its discretion in this respect by prior commitments or understandings with the public"* (p. 5).

Sarratt v. Cash,
103 S.C. 531, 88 S.E. 256 (1916)
(Decided by the Supreme Court of South Carolina)

[This was an action to enjoin a board of education from locating a school building on a certain site near the center of the district. Plaintiffs alleged that those who circulated the petition upon which an election for approving a bond issue was ordered, "represented to the electors that the new building would be located in the west end" of the district, and that but for this representation the bond issue would not have been approved. For violating this alleged understanding, they attempted to enjoin the board.]

HYDRICK, J. . . .

.   .   .   .

Assuming . . . as we must for the purpose of this inquiry, that the representations were made with the effect alleged, the question is: Should that preclude the trustees from now exercising the judgment and discretion vested in them by law to locate the building where they believed it ought to be located to best subserve the educational interests of the district as a whole? Or, stating the proposition differently, must they now, because of those representations, abuse their discretion by locating the building where, in their judgment, it will not be for the best interests of the district? They are bound, under the statute and their oath of office, to exercise their discretion and judgment, in the language of the statute (Civ. Code, § 1761) "so as best to promote the educational interests of their district." This power and duty is continuing and inalienable. They could not, therefore, bind themselves by promises or representation, so as to divest themselves of the right to a free and untrammeled exercise of their judgment and discretion for the best interests of their district at the time they were required to act as a body. . . . It would be contrary to public policy to allow public officers who are charged with the duty of exercising their judgment and discretion for the benefit of the whole district to bind or fetter themselves by promise or representation to individuals or to electors of a section of the district so that they could not, at all times, act freely and impartially for the benefit of the whole district. The power was conferred upon them for public purposes, and it could not be lawfully bartered away to influence signatures to the petition or votes in the election. The electors are presumed to have known this. Therefore they had no legal right to rely upon the alleged representations, or to be influenced by them in signing the petition or in voting in the election.

Guides for Class Discussion

1. Do you think the ends of equity and justice were served in this case? Give reasons.
2. On what ground did the court arrive at its decision?

25. "Authority of a school board to build school buildings carries with it, by implication, authority to employ architects" (p. 5).

PEOPLE EX REL. KIEHM V. BOARD OF EDUCATION,
190 N.Y.S. 798, 198 App. Div. 476 (1921)
(Decided by the Supreme Court, Appellate Division,
Fourth Department, New York)

[This was an action brought to collect a bill for architectural services from a school board. The board had employed the architect but, when he presented his bill, the board disapproved it on the basis of an opinion of the corporation counsel that it was not legal. This opinion was based, in part, on the fact there was no statutory authority granting to boards the authority to employ architects, although they did have the authority to construct new buildings.]

HUBBS, J. . . .

. . . .

It is quite apparent from the petition and return . . . that the board did not disallow the claim upon its merits, but based its refusal to allow it upon the ground that it was not a legal claim. . . .

. . . .

Undoubtedly the board, having the power and authority to build a new building, had power and authority to employ architects to draw the necessary plans and to make the necessary estimates and specifications. Without such services the board could not make out its estimates of the cost of the proposed building. The board, acting within its authority, did, by resolution, employ the relators who furnished plans, estimates, and specifications which were used by the board in preparing the proposition to submit to prospective bidders. The board then refused to audit the relators' claim upon the ground that it did not have the legal right so to do. It says that the contract with the relators was void, prohibited by subdivision 8 of section 875, aforesaid, and unenforceable, as the amount involved was over $1,000 and the board did not advertise for estimates. It is clear that the section referred to does not apply to a situation like this involving professional services.

Guides for Class Discussion

1. Are you in agreement with the court's reasoning? Give reasons.

2. Compare this decision with the one in *Cobb* v. *Pasadena City Board of Education, infra.*

26. *"In employing an architect, a school board need not resort to competitive bidding in the absence of statute to the contrary"* (p. 5).

Cobb v. Pasadena City Board of Education,
134 Cal. App. 93, 285 P. (2d) 41 (1955)
(Decided by the District Court of Appeal,
Second District, Division 2, California)

[The facts of the case will be found in the material quoted.]

Moore, Presiding Judge.

The question here presented is whether a board of education is required to advertise for competitive bids before it may contract with an architect for his professional services to prepare plans for the city's school extension program.

By his complaint, appellant sought an injunction to prevent respondent from disbursing public funds as architect's fees for services rendered and to be performed in connection with the proposed Pasadena school extension program. . . .

. . . .

The contention here made has long since been denied judicially and legislatively. It has been held that because an architect is an artist, that his work requires taste, skill and technical learning and ability of a rare kind, it would be bad judgment to advertise and get many bids when the lowest bidder might be also the least capable and most inexperienced and his bid absolutely unacceptable and therefore "the employment of a person who is highly and technically skilled in his science or profession is one which may properly be made without competitive bidding." . . . Because all contracts for the construction of improvements must be subject to competitive bidding, and because such contracts must conform with the procedure prescribed in sections 18051 and 18052, supra, it does not follow that in the employment of an architect to prepare plans for a public building a board must comply with those sections. . . . Where competitive proposals do not produce an advantage, a statute requiring competitive bidding does not apply. . . .

. . . .

The contention that respondent improperly employed architects who neither reside in Pasadena nor do business there is based on no authority. . . . Such employment, therefore, lies within the discretion of the board, with which courts will not interfere in the absence of fraud or abuse of discretion in the exercise of its legislative powers. . . .

Guides for Class Discussion

1. What line of reasoning motivated the court?
2. Do you think its reasoning is sound? Give reasons.

27. *"Contracts with architects, like all other contracts, must be made by the board in its corporate capacity and not by an individual member or committee of the board"* (p. 5).

DIERKS SPECIAL SCHOOL DISTRICT v. VAN DYKE,
152 Ark. 26, 237 S.W. 428 (1922)
(Decided by the Supreme Court of Arkansas)

[This was an action by an architect to recover fees allegedly due him from a board of education for services in preparing plans for and supervising the construction of a school building. At issue was the legality of the contract, which it was not shown was either voted by the board or ratified by it while acting in its corporate capacity. The court held the contract was illegal.]

HART, J. . . . It is settled in this state that no contract can be made by a school board except at a board meeting, and that no meeting can be held unless all the directors are present, or the absent member, or members, have been duly notified. It has been further held that notice of a regular meeting is, however, unnecessary where regular meetings are held at stated times fixed by the board. . . . This is in application of the general rule that where persons are authorized by statute to perform a public service, as a board or as an organized body, which requires deliberation, they must be convened in a body that they may have the advice of every member, although they may not all be of the same opinion as to the matter in hand.

While there is in the record in the present case a contract signed by Van Dyke and the president and secretary of the Dierks special school district, employing him as architect in the construction of a new school building, it is not shown that this contract was authorized at a regular meeting of the school board, or at a special meeting where all the directors were present, or where each of them had been duly notified of the meeting. In the application of the rule above stated it is conceded by counsel for the plaintiff, Van Dyke, that he is not entitled to recover on the contract just referred to, but it is claimed by him that the contract in question was ratified by the members of the school board, and that therefore he is entitled to recover upon it just as if it had been legally executed in the first instance.

. . . .

. . . The record shows that on the 4th day of September, 1918, at a meeting of the school board in which four members were present, the board voted to receive the contract presented by the architect, V. B. Van Dyke, and instructed the president and secretary of the school board to sign the same, and that the president and secretary did so. There is nothing to show, however, that this was at a regular meeting of the school board, or that all the members of the board were duly notified to be present at it. It will be noted that two of the members were absent, and it is not shown that they received any notification whatever to be present. This is the only evidence in the record from which to find that the board of directors of said special school district ratified the contract which its president and secretary made with Van Dyke, and this testimony is not sufficient to show a ratification of the contract. As we have already seen, such a contract could only be made or ratified by the board at a regular meeting, or at a call meeting of which all the members of the board were present or had been given due notice.

Guides for Class Discussion

1. On what basis did the court arrive at its decision?
2. Do you think the reasoning of the court was sound? Give reasons.
3. What are the implications of this case for school administration?

28. *"It is well settled that, where an architect agrees to furnish plans and specifications for a building that can be built at a cost closely approximating a given amount, or not to exceed a certain sum, he cannot recover under the contract unless the building he designs can be erected for the sum stipulated, or unless the increased cost is due to some special circumstance"* (p. 5).

PIERCE v. BOARD OF EDUCATION,
211 N.Y.S. 788, 125 Misc. Rep. 589 (1925)
(Decided by the Supreme Court, Orleans County, New York)

[Plaintiffs—architects—brought this action to recover for services rendered defendant "pursuant to an agreement for furnishing preliminary studies, general plans, and specifications for the construction" of two schoolhouses. After completing plans, plaintiffs informed defendant that the elementary-school building could, they thought, be built within the amount of $20,000 and that the combination junior high and elementary building could be constructed for about $75,000. After bids were opened, it was found that the lowest bid for the grade-school building was $38,413, and for the combination building, $101,651.09. Therefore the defendant abandoned the project, and plaintiffs brought this action. They contended that they were entitled to three and one-half per cent of the lowest bids. Defendant contended that it was the duty of plaintiffs to furnish plans so that the building project could be carried out within the appropriation previously voted by the district, the amount of which the plaintiffs knew or should have known.]

EDWARD R. O'MALLEY, J. . . .

. . . .

It seems to be well settled that, where plans are required for a building not to cost more than a certain sum, or are accepted on condition that it can be erected for a given amount, there can be no recovery by the architect, unless the building can be erected for the sum named, or unless the increased cost is due to special circumstances, or to a change of plans by direction of the owner. . . .

In the instant case there was no express stipulation made by the defendant limiting the cost of the buildings to be constructed, but it is claimed that, where the employer is a municipal corporation, as in the case at bar, such a provision is implied in the contract of employment, and this claim is based on the general rule of law that one dealing with the agent of a municipal corporation has no right to presume that the agent is acting within the line of his or its authority, and that it is the duty of one so dealing to ascertain the nature and extent of the agent's authority to contract, and that there were certain specific limitations in the Education Law on the defendant's authority and power to contract for the construction of school buildings, among which was that the expense of the buildings must be within the appropriation voted by the district, and that plaintiffs were bound to know these limitations as a matter of law, and that in fact they did know of these express limitations. . . .

.   .   .   .

The resolution voted upon by the district expressly provided that the total cost of the sites and the buildings was not to exceed $125,000, and the plaintiffs were bound under the law to know that the erection of the buildings and their right to recover under their contract were conditioned on the expense coming within the appropriation. The bids submitted show that the costs would have exceeded the appropriation. The sum of the lowest bids received was 47 per cent. higher than plaintiffs' estimate of the cost of the buildings. The result was that the defendant could not erect the buildings within the appropriation or the estimate given by the plaintiffs, or for a sum that would reasonably approximate the appropriation or the estimate. This being so, the defendant had no power to proceed with the building portion of the project. . . .

.   .   .   .

The limitation contained in the resolution as to costs was binding on both the plaintiffs and the defendant, and I am of the opinion that all of the limitations upon the authority of the defendant to deal with the plaintiffs must be read into and made a part of the contract. If these conclusions are correct, the plaintiffs cannot recover for their services . . . because of a failure on their part to perform the contract.

Guides for Class Discussion

1. Compare the decision in this case with the ones in *Fiske* v. *School District, infra*; and *Ritter* v. *School District, infra*.
2. Are you in agreement with the court? Give reasons.

29. *"Some courts hold—and their decisions appear to be the most reasonable—that a contract between a school board and an architect to prepare general drawings and specifications for a school building is valid even though the board may not, at the time, have the necessary funds to build the building and the building may never be built"* (pp. 5-6).

FISKE v. SCHOOL DISTRICT,
59 Neb. 51, 80 N.W. 265 (1899)
(Decided by the Supreme Court of Nebraska)

[The facts of this case will be found in that portion of the decision which is included herein.]

HARRISON, C. J. . . .
In this action the plaintiff sought a recovery for services alleged to have been rendered to the defendant in preparing plans, drawings, and specifications for school buildings, pursuant to the terms of a contract between the parties. . . .
For a statement of the case, we refer to the former opinion. It need not be repeated here. It will be noticed that the controverted questions relate mainly, if not entirely, to the right of the plaintiff to recover for preliminary plans, drawings, and specifications, which were not used or followed in the construction of any buildings. . . . It is asserted . . . that the authority of school-district boards or officers to contract in regard to erection of buildings or any subject which will or does involve the expenditure of money is limited by statute, and must be within the statutory terms; that it must be within the funds provided or on hand to meet the proposed expenditures; and that the party who contracts with the board or officers does so at his peril, and must take notice of its or their requisite authority or the lack thereof. . . . The projected buildings were never erected; the preliminary plans and drawings could not be said to be a part of any construction of buildings; and, if not, the expense of them was not any part of a building, or necessarily to be paid from a building fund. They were ordered for the use of the district, and were necessary as much so as many other articles or services which come within the general expenses of a school district, and must be paid for from the general fund. There is a fund from which all such expenses are paid, and we may call it a "general fund." It is so recognized and designated in the general school law, and payments directed to be made from it. Comp. St. c. 79, subd. 4, § 13. There was a legitimate expense and charge against the district, and funds from which it could be properly paid. The facts of this case, as stated in the petition, place it clearly without the direct terms or the principle of the cases cited, to which we have hereinbefore referred.

Guides for Class Discussion

1. Compare this case with *Ritter* v. *School District, infra*. With which do you agree? Give reasons.
2. What line of reasoning did the court follow in arriving at its decision?

30. *"Some courts take the position . . . that a contract between a school board and an architect is invalid where the plans and specifications call for a building which would cost more than the board could legally spend for that purpose"* (p. 6).

RITTER v. SCHOOL DISTRICT,
291 Pa. 439, 140 A. 126 (1928)
(Decided by the Supreme Court of Pennsylvania)

[This was an action by an architect to recover his commission "on a school building which was never built, and for which he did not even prepare definite and finished plans."]

SCHAFFER, J. . . .

. . . .

The insurmountable block in plaintiff's way to recovery is that what he contemplated would result in an unlawful increase in the indebtedness of the school district. It had but $417,000 available for the building. His plan contemplated an expenditure of $800,000. Such an outlay the school board could not have made. The case at bar differs from Sauer v. McKees Rocks School Dist., 243 Pa. 295, 90 A. 150, in which an architect sued for commissions for services in connection with a school building and where the cost of the structure exceeded the 2 per cent. borrowing capacity of the district. There the architect originally claimed commissions on the completed cost of the building. By leave of court he amended his claim so as to recover only for the services actually performed, and he was permitted to recover that amount. Had the plaintiff here made a like claim, which on the trial he expressly declined to do, he might have succeeded.

Appellant's counsel argue that his contract was separate from that for the erection of the building and in itself did not exhaust the borrowing capacity of the school district. With this we do not agree. Plaintiff's contract was inseparably bound up with the whole building program, and by express reference made a part of it. When he planned a building as part of the program for which it was beyond the power of the defendant to contract, he could not recover his commissions on the cost of it.

Guides for Class Discussion

1. Are you in agreement with the decision in this case? Give reasons.
2. Compare the decision in this case with the ones in *Fiske* v. *School District, supra,* and *Pierce* v. *Board of Education, supra.*

31. "Where a school board breaks a contract with an architect, the rule is that he is entitled to recover the contract price, less whatever payments have been made and less what it would cost him to perform the contract" (p. 6).

PAGE V. HARLINGEN INDEPENDENT SCHOOL DISTRICT,
23 S.W. (2d) 829 (Tex.) (1929)
(Decided by the Court of Civil Appeals of Texas)

[In this case a school board entered into a contract with an architect to draw plans for and supervise the construction of three school buildings. After two had been completed, the board repudiated its contract covering the third. To recover for the alleged wrongful and illegal repudiation of the contract, the architect brought this action. The first question before the court was the legality of the contract. Having decided it was legal, the next question the court was called upon to answer was the amount plaintiff was entitled to recover.]

COBBS, J. . . .

. . . .

. . . we think the facts establish a valid contract for all the work done by appellants, and that the act of the school board in setting aside appellants' contract and giving it to another violated the contractual relation existing between the appellants and appellee.

. . . .

On account of the breach of the contract by appellee under the circumstances, appellants are entitled to recover damages; the contract price less what appellee district has paid them, and less the amount it would cost appellants to carry out their contract. Gould v. McCormick, 75 Wash. 61, 134 P. 676, 47 L. R. A. (N. S.) 765, Ann. Cas. 1915 A, 710; Jacobberger v. School District, 122 Or. 124, 256 P. 652; Phelps v. Connellee (Tex. Com. App.) 285 S.W. 1047; Id. (Civ. App.) 278 S.W. 939.

In the Jacobberger and Gould Cases, supra, the rule stated is: "The damages for wrongfully discharging an architect who had undertaken to draw plans for and superintend the construction of a building for a percentage of its cost are the difference between the contract price and what it would have cost them to complete their undertaking at the time of their discharge." On motion for a rehearing in the Phelps v. Connellee Case, supra, the appeals court modified this holding to the extent that a further deduction of whatever amount the architect may have saved himself by finding other employment should be made from the recovery. But the Supreme Court reversed the Court of Civil Appeals' opinion as rendered on rehearing, and held that an architect wrongfully discharged is entitled to recover his contract price, less whatever payments have been made, and what it would cost him to perform his contract; and that such further mitigation of damages was a matter of defense to be pleaded by the defendant.

. . . .

Appellants have shown a legal right to recover the sum of $8,033.52, therefore the judgment of the trial court is reversed, and judgment here rendered for appellants for the said sum of $8,033.52.

Reversed and rendered.

Guides for Class Discussion

1. Do you think the rule laid down by the court for determining the amount of damages to which the architect was entitled was equitable? Give reasons.
2. Do you think a court today would follow this same rule?
3. Had the contract been illegal, how much damages could the architect have recovered?

32. *"Where the statutes do not require school boards to let build-ing contracts on the basis of competitive bidding, a school board may or may not, at its discretion, advertise for bids"* (p. 6).

Smith v. Board of Education,
405 Ill. 143, 89 N.E. (2d) 893 (1950)
(Decided by the Supreme Court of Illinois)

[This was an action to restrain a board of education from proceed-ing with a contract for the construction of a new high school build-ing. Among other things, plaintiff contended the contract was illegal because it was not based upon competitive bidding. The lower court ruled in favor of the defendant, and the higher court affirmed its decision.]

Simpson, Justice.

. . . .

The legislature has provided for the creation of boards of education and has delegated to such boards the power to build schoolhouses, upon receiv-ing authority to do so from a majority of the electorate of the school dis-trict, subject to the approval of the county superintendent of schools respecting certain health and safety measures. . . . The method to be employed in letting contracts for the construction of school buildings has been left to the discretion of the school boards of the respective school districts. Appellant attacks the wisdom of permitting the board of education of a high school district to negotiate contracts for building schoolhouses without limitation as to size, cost, or methods to be employed in the letting of such contracts. It is insisted that the unrestrained acts of the board of education, in such cases, is contrary to public policy. Where no limitation has been placed upon a school board by the vote of the people of the district, it has the right to use its discretion as to the character and cost of a school building which shall be adequate and proper for the use of the district. . . .

The remaining question to be determined is whether the allegations of the complaint are sufficient to charge the Board of Education with fraud in awarding the construction contract to Arnold Lies Company, Inc. While the words, "fraud," "fraudulently," and "conspiracy," are used repeatedly, a careful reading of the complaint compels the conclusion that these charges are based on two main allegations, first, that the Board of Educa-tion eliminated competitive bidding, and second, that the contract was awarded for a substantially larger sum than might have been bid by other contractors. In the absence of allegations of facts showing fraudulent acts or conduct in connection with the awarding of the contract, this was not sufficient to charge fraud. We have already pointed out that the legislature delegated the authority to build schoolhouses, under proper circumstances, to boards of education without requiring that contracts for their construction be awarded as a result of competitive bidding. Where the language used in a statute is plain and certain it must be given effect by the courts and we cannot legislate but must interpret the law as announced by the legislature.

Guides for Class Discussion

1. Are you in agreement with this decision? Give reasons.
2. Compare this case with *Coward* v. *Mayor, etc., of City of Bayonne, infra.*

33. "*. . . the board may reject all bids unless its advertisement is so worded as to constitute an offer to accept the lowest bid*" (*p. 6*).

Coward v. Mayor, etc., of City of Bayonne,
67 N.J.L. 470, 51 A. 490 (1902)
(Decided by the Supreme Court of New Jersey)

[In this case an attempt was made to invalidate a contract for the construction of a school building made by the board of education. The board employed an architect and, after he had finished drawing up the specifications, advertised for bids. In the advertisement the board reserved the right to reject all bids. Following the rejection of the bids, new specifications were drawn up and the contract again was submitted for bidding. In awarding the contract, certain changes were made in the specifications from those included in the architect's drawings. On the ground that the contract was illegal, this action was brought to restrain the board from proceeding as it planned to do. The court held the contract was legal.]

GARRETSON, J. . . .

. . . .

The board of education of Bayonne are not required by the charter of that city, or by any general law of the state, to advertise for proposals for doing any of the work which they are authorized to do. The only provision is in section 91 of the charter, supra, and, although the board did actually advertise for proposals, they were not required to award the contract to the lowest bidder; and the award of the contract to a higher or the highest bidder, or to some one who did not bid at all, would not, in the absence of bad faith and corruption, be regarded as such an abuse of that discretion conferred upon them by law as to justify interference by this court. The employment of an architect to prepare plans and specifications, and the soliciting of bids, may have been a proper method of ascertaining the most favorable contract that could be obtained for the city. It is the method which a private person would pursue as to his own affairs. And after the bids had been received there was nothing to prevent the board from so modifying the specifications that a better contract might be made for the city. The board had the right to purchase for use in the building any article or apparatus of a specific make, even though it was patented or the product of an exclusive manufacture. City of Newark v. Bonnell, 57 N. J. Law, 424, 31 Atl. 408. Nor do we think that a statement in the advertisement that only union labor should be employed (such a condition not being contained in the contract) would vitiate the contract. The evidence fails to disclose that the board of education had any motive in awarding the contract, other than that of making the best bargain possible for the city. We think that they exercised the discretion conferred upon them by law with good faith and honesty.

Guides for Class Discussion

1. On what basis did the court arrive at its decision? Was this sound?

2. Compare this decision with the one rendered in *Smith* v. *Board of Education, supra.*

3. Had the advertisement for bids not included the statement that the board reserved the right to reject all bids, would the court have held as it did?

34. "*In case the statutes require school boards to advertise for bids on school-building contracts and to award such contracts to the lowest responsible bidder, the mode of making the contract is the measure of the board's power to make it, and if the statute is disregarded, the contractor cannot recover on the contract*" (p. 6).

Yoder v. School District of Luzerne Township,
399 Pa. 425, 160 A. (2d) 419 (1960)
(Decided by the Supreme Court of Pennsylvania)

[In this case a contractor brought an action against a school district to recover for work done and supplies and materials furnished in connection with the paving of certain school playgrounds. Plaintiff was low bidder on a contract for the paving job and was awarded the contract. Specifications called for 4,379 square yards of six-inch base, at a total cost of $29,882.45. The contract stated no extra work would be done unless so ordered in writing. Without complying with the statute respecting advertising and bidding, the area surfaced by plaintiff was increased to 10,240 yards and the base was changed from six inches to four. These changes were made pursuant to oral orders of the board members "who singly or in groups, visited the job sites from time to time." The final bill was for $44,174.60 instead of the $29,882.45 originally agreed upon. Plaintiff received $29,174.60 and brought this action to recover the $15,000 which he contended was still due him. The district's refusal to pay was based upon its contention that the extra work had not been performed in conformity with the statute requiring public advertisement for bids and formal corporate action in the letting of the bids. The trial court sustained the defendant district's position and the contractor appealed. The higher court upheld the lower court's decision.]

Benjamin R. Jones, Justice.

· · · · · · · · · · · · · · · · · ·

These sections [of the statute relating to bidding and the method of contracting] are mandatory, not directory. Similar provisions in other statutes have been uniformly construed as mandatory. . . . This Court said in Commonwealth v. Zang, 142 P. Super 566, 571, 16 A. 2d 741; 744: ". . . the purpose and public policy behind these provisions of the School Code are to protect the school district from any possible collusion and dishonesty, and to insure that where material or supplies . . . are purchased they will be obtained at the best possible price. . . . To permit contracts to be entered into and expenditures made without compliance with the provisions of the act would defeat the very object the legislature had in mind in inserting them. In re Summit Hill School Directors, [258 Pa. 575, 102 A. 278]. . . ." "The infirmities of human nature, the natural disposition to favor friends, personal and political, and the various motives which influence public officers to depart from a strict and rigid adherence to the obligations that rest upon them . . . should be held strictly within the limits of the powers conferred upon them.": Smith v. City of Philadelphia, 227 Pa. 423, 76 A. 221, 223.

In Luzerne Township v. County of Fayette, 330 Pa. 247, 251, 199 A. 327, 329, we said "All contracts by county commissioners involving an expenditure exceeding $100 must be in writing. Act of June 27, 1895, P. L. 403, § 10 as amended . . . and embodied in the General County Law of May 2, 1929, P. L. 1278, § 348 . . . . This provision of the law is not merely directory, but mandatory, and a contract which does not comply with it imposes no liability upon the county. Where a statute prescribes the formal mode of making public contracts it must be observed; otherwise they cannot be enforced against the governmental agency involved. . . ."

Guides for Class Discussion

1. Are you in agreement with the court's thinking? Give reasons.
2. See *Reams* v. *Cooley, infra.*

35. *"In case the statutes require [competitive bidding] . . . the mode of making the contract is the measure of the board's power . . . , and if the statute is disregarded . . . the contractor cannot recover on quantum meruit, in a court of equity, the actual value of the building"* (p. 6).

REAMS v. COOLEY,
171 Cal. 150, 152 P. 293 (1915)
(Decided by the Supreme Court of California)

[In this case a contract for plastering had been let without bidding, as required by statute. Upon its completion, the board refused to pay the contractor, on the ground the contract had been made improperly, and he brought this action. The court held in favor of the district, and the contractor appealed.]

LORIGAN, J. . . .

. . . .

. . . While under sections 1617 and 1674 of the Political Code authority is given to school trustees to erect school buildings, there is at the same time by subdivision 22 of section 1617, applicable alike to boards of trustees of union high school districts as to boards of trustees of common school districts, a mode prescribed for exercising that power. By that subdivision where the work (as here) is to exceed the sum of $200, a valid contract can only be entered into with the lowest bidder on competitive bidding after published notice therefor. . . . No contract, either expressly or impliedly, could be entered into by the school board except with the lowest bidder after advertisement, and, of course, *no implied liability to pay upon a quantum meruit could exist where the prohibition of the statute against contracting in any other manner than as prescribed is disregarded.* [Emphasis supplied.]

It is urged in this case, as it invariably is in all such cases, that the application of this rule works a great hardship if the school district may retain the benefit of the work of the contractor and be relieved of liability to compensate him therefor. But the provision of the law limiting the power of school boards to validly contract, except in a prescribed mode, proceeds from a consideration of public policy not peculiar to such boards, but adopted as the policy of the state with reference to inferior boards and public bodies, and it would be difficult to perceive what practical public benefit or result could accrue by legislative limitation or prohibition on the power of such bodies to contract if courts were to allow a recovery where the limitation or prohibition is disregarded; in fact, the plea of hardship urged here was answered in the Zottman case [20 Cal. 96] by language as pertinent now as it was then, where the court said:

"It may sometimes seem a hardship upon a contractor that all compensation for work done, etc., should be denied him; but it should be remembered that he, no less than the officers of the corporation, when he deals in a matter expressly provided for in the charter, is bound to see to it that the charter is complied with. If he neglect this, or choose to take the hazard, he is a mere volunteer, and suffers only what he ought to have anticipated. If the statute forbids the contract which he has made, he knows it, or ought to know it, before he places his money or services at hazard."

Guides for Class Discussion

1. Are you in agreement with the court's reasoning? Give reasons.
2. Compare this decision with the one in *White River School Township* v. *Dorrell, infra.*
3. Compare this decision with the one rendered in *Yoder* v. *School District of Luzerne Township, supra.*

36. *"In order to have competitive bidding, plans and specifications must be sufficiently definite to enable those who bid to bid on a common basis; otherwise there is no competition"* (p. 6).

Homan v. Board of Education,
3 N.J.M. 301, 127 A. 824 (1925)
(Decided by the Supreme Court of New Jersey)

[This was an action to set aside the award of a contract by a school board.]

Per Curiam. The writ of certiorari was issued to review the action of the defendant in awarding the contract for the erection of a schoolhouse, known as the Rosedale School on the 24th day of September, 1924. The prosecutors' bid, after public advertisement, was $197,330. The defendant's bid was $198,689.

The ground upon which the prosecutors seek to set aside the award of the contract is that it is in violation of the statute which provides:

"All contracts shall be awarded to the lowest responsible bidder." . . .
This provision limits the power of the board. . . .

What constitutes responsibility within the meaning of the statute is
fully discussed and illustrated in the cases of Paterson Contracting Co.
v. City of Hackensack, 122 A. 741; Peluso v. Hoboken, 98 N.J. Law, 706,
126 A 623; Harrington's Sons Co. v. Jersey City, 78 N.J. Law, 610, 75 A.
943.

Under these cases it is not shown in the record that the prosecutors
were not "responsible bidders" within the meaning of the statute, and in
the defendant's brief, it is stated, at the very outset let it be made clear
that the financial responsibility of the H. John Homan Company is not
questioned.

. . . .

The advertising for bids, however, requested that the time be stated
in the contract within which the building would be finished.

As was said by this court in the case of Armitage v. Mayor, etc., of
Newark, 86 N.J. Law, 6, 90 A. 1035, the general vice of this course is
that no common standard for the competition is set up. . . . Testimony
was taken which is urged as a justification of the board's action, viz. that
the prosecutors delayed the completion of prior contracts with the board,
but this is no legal excuse for not complying with the plain mandate of
the statute.

For these reasons the award of the contract in this case is set aside,
with costs.

Guides for Class Discussion

1. Do you think the court acted equitably in ruling that common
   standards for competition must be set up in order to constitute
   responsibility in bidding? Give reasons.
2. See *Yoder* v. *School District of Luzerne Township, supra.*

37. *"Where the statutes require that bids be let to the lowest responsible bidder, in deciding who is the lowest responsible bidder, the board should take into consideration cost, financial standing, experience, resources, and all other factors necessary for it to form a judgment of the bidder's responsibility"* (pp. 6-7).

MEYER V. BOARD OF EDUCATION,
221 N.Y.S. (2d) 500 (1961)
(Decided by the Supreme Court, Special Term,
Nassau County, Part I)

[This was an application for an order to cancel an award of a contract made by the defendant board to Werther Electrical Contracting Co., Inc., and to direct the award of this contract to the plaintiff. Plaintiff was the lowest bidder when bids were solicited, and he contended he should receive the contract. The court held that the record failed to show that defendant was arbitrary in its awarding of the contract.]

MARIO PITTONI, Justice.

. . . .

The basic facts are not in dispute. On Wednesday, August 2, 1961, the bids were received by the Board of Education, and the Board, not being familiar with either of the two bidders involved, and anxious to have the work completed before the fall session began, instructed its architect to immediately investigate and report on each of these bidding contractors. On August 7, 1961 the architect submitted his report to the Board: that he had requested the petitioner to supply the names of architectural firms to which inquiries could be directed concerning recent projects which the petitioner had completed; that the petitioner supplied the names of two architectural firms; that when the school architect communicated with both of these references one responded that the petitioner had done a project for that firm over 10 years prior to the inquiry, and the other said that he would not recommend the petitioner. The second said that although the petitioner had once been a good contractor he had experienced difficulties in the last few years, was having difficulty in getting approval of his work from underwriting laboratories, and that after being awarded an electrical contract as a low bidder he submitted estimates for extra work, which were not included in the plans and specifications, and which were too high in price. The investigating architect also reported that his investigation showed that Werther had a good reputation in the industry for its work and had received the highest recommendation from well-known engineers and architects. Upon the report and recommendation of its architect the Board then proceeded, at its August 7, 1961 public meeting, to award the contract to Werther as the lowest responsible bidder. Another public hearing at the petitioner's request was held on August 28, 1961. The petitioner and his attorney were heard and the Board adhered to its original decision.

The key word in Section 103 of the General Municipal Law and in the decision of the Board is "responsible." Without question it means "accountable" or "reliable." The Board came to its decision that Werther was the lowest responsible bidder after considering the report of its architect who was designated or appointed to seek facts as to the responsibility of the bidders involved. The Board concluded that upon the facts in hand Werther was a responsible bidder and the petitioner was not.

The Board used a common sense approach and method in making its determination and this court cannot say that it was wrong in the method chosen; nor will it define or limit the standards the Board should have used as guides so long as the method chosen was reasonable.

The burden of proof was on the petitioner to show that he was a responsible bidder. There was no burden on the Board to go out and investigate blindly as to the bidder's responsibility. He submitted two persons as references, and upon interview these persons supplied information which failed to show that the petitioner was a responsible person.

. . . .

Accordingly, it cannot be said that the Board was arbitrary, capricious or unreasonable in making its decision. . . .

Guides for Class Discussion

1. Do you think the court would have ruled as it did had the board made the investigation itself, rather than requested the architect to make it? Give reasons.

2. Compare this decision with *Joseph Rugo, Inc.* v. *Henson, infra.*

38. "*Where a school board acts in good faith and its judgment is based upon substantial fact, the courts will not overrule its discretion in determining the lowest responsible bidder*" (p. 7).

JOSEPH RUGO, INC. v. HENSON,
148 Conn. 430, 171 A. (2d) 409 (1961)
(Decided by the Supreme Court of Errors of Connecticut)

[This was an action by a contractor to compel defendant to award to him a contract for the construction of a new high school. Defendant demurred, and the lower court sustained the demurrer. The plaintiff appealed, and the higher court here held that the board, which had reserved the right to reject any and all offers, was justified in rejecting all bids where it felt they were excessive, even if the action was arbitrary and capricious, so long as it was not fraudulent.]

BORDON, Associate Justice.

. . . .

Although there are three assignments of error, the only question to be determined is whether there was error in sustaining the demurrer. On the face of the record, it appears that the court sustained the demurrer on grounds other than those claimed by the defendants. If, however, a proper conclusion was reached, the ruling may be upheld. . . . In passing on a demurrer, the court should consider only the grounds specified. . . . Upon appeal, we consider the whole record and give judgment for the party who, on the whole, appears to be entitled to it. . . .

There is no allegation in the complaint which overcomes the recognized principle of law that where municipalities reserve the right to reject any or all bids they are empowered to do so. . . . It is true that certain paragraphs of the complaint allege arbitrariness, capriciousness, and similar conduct, but such conduct, if there was any, by the empowered officers is immaterial, since the right to reject all bids was asserted in the invitation to bid. . . . Courts have relaxed the application of the established principle of law only where fraud or corruption has influenced the conduct of the officials. No allegation of fraud or corruption appears in this complaint.

All that is required of officials is that they observe good faith and accord all bidders just consideration, thus avoiding favoritism and corruption. An honest exercise of discretion will generally not be disturbed. Courts will only intervene to prevent the rejection of a bid when the obvious purpose of the rejection is to defeat the object and integrity of competitive bidding. . . .

Guides for Class Discussion

1. Do you think the court was right in holding that, as long as the board did not act fraudulently or corruptly, its actions would be upheld in this case? Justify your answer.
2. What did the court have to say, indirectly, concerning the purpose of a competitive-bidding statute?

39. *"The mere passage of a resolution by a board to accept a bid does not constitute a contract—there is no contract until the bidder has been officially notified that his bid has been accepted—and a board may rescind its resolution awarding the contract at any time before such notification"* (p. 7).

WAYNE CROUSE, INC. v. SCHOOL DISTRICT OF BOROUGH OF BRADDOCK,
341 Pa. 497, 19 A. (2d) 843 (1941)
(Decided by the Supreme Court of Pennsylvania)

[In Pennsylvania, where the statute required that building contracts be reduced to writing, a school board, after advertising for bids for plumbing and heating, voted to award the contract to plaintiff, who was the lowest bidder. Later, before the contract was reduced to writing and signed, the board rescinded its action on the ground plaintiff was not the lowest responsible bidder, and this action was brought to compel the board to enter into the contract with plaintiff. The court ruled against plaintiff.]

MAXEY, Justice.

. . . .

The school district through its secretary verbally notified the plaintiff to proceed to execute the written contracts prepared and secure material-men and performance bonds. The officers of Plaintiff Corporation proceeded to do this the morning after the meeting at which the award was made to it. The Plumbers' Union protested to the school board that if the school district persisted in the award, labor difficulties would be experienced. The secretary and architect consulted with the plaintiff corporation's representatives but the latter's efforts with the union were unsuccessful and the school district was so notified.

The following appears on the minutes of the meeting of the Board of Directors of the school district held on March 10, 1938: "It was regularly moved and seconded by Wrobleski and Andolina that the actions of the board in awarding the plumbing contract . . . to Wayne & Crouse, Inc. . . . be rescinded because of the finding after investigation that they are not the lowest responsible bidder, in that they cannot perform the said contract. All ayes. . ." . . . .

. . . .

When a municipal body advertises for bids for public work and receives what appears to be a satisfactory bid, it is within the contemplation of both bidder and acceptor that no contractual relation shall arise therefrom until a written contract embodying all material terms of the offer and acceptance has been formally entered into. The motion whose adoption is evidenced by the minutes of the school district in the instant case meant merely that the proposal was accepted subject to the preparation and execution of a formal contract or subject to the motion being rescinded before the contract was executed. A preliminary declaration of intention to enter into a formal contract, which was all the motion amounted to, did not in any way limit the school directors' freedom of future action.

Guides for Class Discussion

1. Are you in agreement with this decision? Give reasons.
2. What line of reasoning motivated the court?

40. "*If a contractor makes an honest mistake in calculating the cost of a school building and the mistake goes to the essence of the contract, a court of equity will annul the bid and put the parties in statu quo*" (p. 7).

BOARD OF EDUCATION v. HOOPER,
350 S.W. (2d) 629 (Ky.) (1961)
(Decided by the Court of Appeals of Kentucky)

[The facts of this case will be found in the material quoted.]

CULLEN, Commissioner.

Appellees Hooper and Burchett, partners, submitted a bid to the Board of Education of Floyd County for the construction of a school building.

As required by the specifications, the bid was accompanied by a bid bond, with appellee Travelers Indemnity Company as surety, conditioned that if the bid be accepted the bidders would execute a contract for the work in accordance with their bid and the specifications. Upon the opening of the bids the Hooper-Burchett bid, in the amount of $73,978.90, was found to be the lowest and was accepted by the board of education. The following day Hooper and Burchett notified the board that by inadvertence the price of the steel required in the construction, amounting to $12,000, had been omitted from their bid, and by reason thereof they could not execute a contract for their bid price. Three days later, without readvertising for bids, the board let a contract to the next lower bidder, whose bid was $78,000. Thereafter the board brought this action against Hooper and Burchett and the surety on their bid bond, seeking to recover the amount of the bond (which was five percent of the bid price). The court entered judgment for the defendants and the board has appealed.

Hooper and Burchett testified that the mistake in their bid arose from the fact that they had divided between them the work of preparing the bid estimates and each had assumed that the other had included the price of the steel in his estimates.

The facts in this case cannot be distinguished from those in Board of Regents of Murray State Normal School v. Cole, 209 Ky. 761, 273 S.W. 508, where in submitting a bid of $207,787 the bidder by inadvertence omitted the cost of cut stone in the amount of $21,066. It was held that the bidder was entitled to be relieved from his bid . . . .

. . . The rationale of the case is that even though the mistake is unilateral, the bidder may be relieved from his contract if the mistake is one of material substance and of such consequence that enforcement of the contract would be unconscionable; if the mistake involved mere ordinary negligence and not gross carelessness; if the other party will suffer no damage other than the loss of the bargain; and if the bidder gives prompt notice of the mistake.

. . . The fact that notice of the mistake is not given until after acceptance of the bid will not preclude relief. . . . .

It is our opinion that the trial court properly denied recovery on the bid bond.

. . . .

The judgment is affirmed.

Guides for Class Discussion

1. On what ground did the court arrive at its decision?
2. As a result of this decision, could one who had been the low bidder change his mind and thereby avoid his obligation?

41. "After bids have been accepted, courts will permit minor, but not major, changes in the specifications. . ." (p. 7).

HIBBS V. ARENSBERG,
276 Pa. 24, 119 A. 727 (1923)
(Decided by the Supreme Court of Pennsylvania)

[This was an action to restrain a board of education from carrying out a contract for the construction of a school building that was let to one who was not the lowest bidder. Among other things, it was charged that the architect's specifications regarding materials were not sufficiently definite so as to insure that all bidders were bidding on the same basis, and that changes in the specifications were made after the contract was let. In arriving at its decision, the court commented on the effect of modifying or changing the specifications after a bid has been accepted.]

KEPHART, J. . . .

  . . . .

It is averred, in the bill to restrain the school directors from awarding the contract to construct a badly needed school building in a school district in Fayette county, that the architect's plans and specifications do not fully state the kind, quality, and quantity of materials required. One special item reads:

"The face brick . . . to be a thoroughly vitrified, wire-cut, face brick of such color as will be selected by the architect and school board; . . . to cost not more than $34.00 per thousand."

We see no reason why an intelligent bid could not be made on this item. Vitrified, wire-cut, face brick has a definite meaning; the contract preserved the right of inspection and rejection of materials; and there was little opportunity to slight the quality. If a certain make of brick had been selected, or several makes, we can readily see a charge of a different character might be presented.

That the directors later decided to use a little more expensive brick would not condemn the letting, or cause the directors to be liable for the increased price, or avoid the purchase. There was no such departure from the general purpose as would require reletting. Unforeseen contingencies or new ideas sometimes make it necessary to change the character or quality of material or a part of a structure from the original plans. A certain flexibility in the power of officials to take care of these matters is intended to be granted, that the law relating to public letting may not become an instrument of oppression through a too rigid construction. These officers must act honestly, reasonably, and intelligently, and a new departure must not so vary from the original plan or be of such importance as to constitute a new undertaking, which the act controls, and where fairness could only be reached through competitive bidding. Courts, however, will be slow to interfere unless it appears the officers are not acting in good faith.

Guides for Class Discussion

1. What conditions must prevail for the courts to approve the making of minor changes in specifications after a contract has been let?
2. Do you think this decision represents "good" law? Give reasons.

42. *"In some states a school district will not be bound under an ultra vires contract even though it retains and enjoys the use of property obtained under such a contract"* (p. 7).

HONEY CREEK SCHOOL TOWNSHIP v. BARNES,
119 Ind. 213, 21 N.E. 747 (1889)
(Decided by the Supreme Court of Indiana)

[The facts of this case will be found in that part of the decision reproduced.]

OLDS, J. This action is brought by the appellees against the appellant. The complaint is in one paragraph, and alleges that on the 1st day of February, 1884, one Benjamin King, at that time the legal and acting school trustee of said school township, bought of the plaintiffs books for the use of the schools of said township; that said books were received and used by the schools of said township, and that the same were necessary for such township in its schools, and for the price of $56.25; that upon said date said trustee, as such, executed to the plaintiffs, in the firm name and style of A. S. Barnes & Co., his written obligation to pay the same out of the special school fund of said township on or before the 20th day of January . . . . It further averred that George W. Kemp was elected trustee as the successor of King, and a refusal to pay the amount. . . . Appellant filed a demurrer to the complaint, which was overruled and the ruling assigned as error. The question presented is as to whether a township school trustee has authority to purchase school books and bind the school township for the payment of the same.

It is contended by counsel for appellee that section 4444, Rev. St. 1881, authorizes the township trustee to purchase necessary school books for the schools of his township. So much of said section as is material in the consideration of this case is as follows: "The trustees shall take charge of the educational affairs of their respective townships, towns, and cities. They shall employ teachers, establish and locate conveniently a sufficient number of schools for the education of the white children therein, and build or otherwise provide suitable houses, furniture, apparatus, and other articles and educational appliances necessary for the thorough organization and efficient management of said schools." . . .

The uncontroverted evidence in the case shows the books purchased to be 75 copies of Monteith's Popular Science Readers; that they were used by the pupils in their reading exercises, as contended by counsel, "to give the pupils a change in reading exercises, to draw out new thoughts, and an additional incentive to new exertion." The same could be said of any new readers or text-books purchased by the trustee and put in use in the schools. They would produce a change and stimulate the mind and divert the line of thought from the subjects in the old books, but it must be admitted, and it is too plain to require argument to demonstrate the proposition, that if the trustee has the authority to purchase this class of books he may purchase any other readers, spelling-books, or any other class of text-books; that he may supply all the text-books used in the schools of his township at the expense of his school township. This may be the proper system for our state to adopt. That is not for us here to determine, but the trustees cannot pursue such a course and bind the school township without some further legislation on the subject. . . . School townships are corporations with limited statutory powers, and all who deal with a trustee of a school township are charged with notice of the scope of his authority, and that he can bind his township only by such contracts as are authorized by law. . . .

The fact that the books were received by the trustee, and used under his direction, creates no liability. . . .

Guides for Class Discussion

1. Compare this decision with the one rendered in *White River School Township* v. *Dorrell, infra*. Which do you think represents the "better" law? Give reasons.

2. Considering the date of this decision—1889—do you think it would still be followed in some jurisdictions?

3. What is the rationale of this decision?

43. *"The courts in some states . . . hold that a district must pay for property retained and used under an ultra vires contract"* (p. 7).

WHITE RIVER SCHOOL TOWNSHIP V. DORRELL,
26 Ind. App. 538, 59 N.E. 867 (1901)
(Decided by the Appellate Court of Indiana)

[The facts of the case will be found in the material which follows].

ROBINSON, J. . . .

On August 4, 1896, appellant's [school district's] trustee was engaged in erecting a suitable and necessary school house in a certain school district having about 40 children of school age, and having no suitable school house. The contract price of the building was $1,300. The township had no funds belonging to the special school fund with which to pay for the completion of the building, and it required $500 to complete the building. The trustee represented to appellee that it was necessary for him to have such sum, and at the trustee's request, and for the purpose of completing the building, appellee turned over to the trustee that sum, which was used in paying for the erection of the building under the contract, and was paid by the trustee to the contractor for the purpose of paying for the completion of the building, and the township since that time and now retains the benefit derived from the use of such sum in the use of such school house for school purposes. Such sum was not in excess of the fund on hand to which the debt is chargeable and the fund derived from the tax assessed for the year 1896. The trial court held that appellee ought to be subrogated to the rights of the contractor to the extent of $500 with interest.

The right of subrogation is not founded upon contract, express or implied. It is based upon the principles of equity and justice, and includes every instance where one party, not a mere volunteer, pays for another a debt for which the latter was primarily liable, and which in good conscience and equity he should have paid. . . . The findings show that the money received by the trustee was paid out by him for property actually received by the school corporation and retained by it. The contract for building the house was such a contract as the trustee was authorized to make. The money was advanced to the trustee for the purpose of completing a necessary and suitable school house. The trustee had not the means in hand to complete the building, and the money advanced was, in fact, applied to that purpose. To permit a recovery in such a case is in no way recognizing a general power in the trustee to borrow money.

There is no suggestion whatever of any fraud in the building of the house. Appellant has received and retains the benefit of the money so advanced, and the simplest principles of equity and justice require that it should repay it. . . .

Guides for Class Discussion

1. What is meant by "subrogation"?
2. On what grounds does the court justify its reasoning?
3. Are you in agreement with the court's thinking?
4. Do you think the court would have held as it did had there been fraud involved, or had the trustee not been possessed of the authority to build the building?

44. *"If a school board makes a contract for the erection of a school building or for the purchase of other school property which it had no authority to make, it cannot later ratify the contract by any act of its own so as to make it binding on the board"* (p. 7).

School Directors v. Fogelman,
76 Ill. 189 (1875)
(Decided by the Supreme Court of Illinois)

[This was an action by the successors of certain school directors, against the directors of a school district questioning the validity of three orders which they had drawn in favor of defendant. Each order was purported to be in part payment for the construction of a school house. It was contended that the directors had acted illegally, since no vote of the electors had been taken on the matter as required by statute.]

Mr. Justice Breese delivered the opinion of the Court:
.   .   .   .

It is conceded no vote of the people of the district was had authorizing the building of this school house. The orders purport, on their face, to be for such purpose, and it was no difficult matter for any person about negotiating them to ascertain if a vote had been taken. The returns of such an election are, by law, made to the town treasurer, the officer on whom they are drawn, and if inquiry had been made of him as to this fact, he would have informed the inquirer, as he testified, that no vote had been taken.

Section 48 of the act of 1865, which was in force when this contract was made, is most explicit. It declares it shall not be lawful for a board of directors to purchase or locate a school house site, or to purchase, build or remove a school house, etc., without a vote of the people, at an election to be called, etc. If this is the lawful course to be pursued, any other course to accomplish the object was necessarily unlawful, and the act null and void. These bodies can exercise no other powers than expressly granted, or such as may be necessary to carry into effect a granted power. Glidden et al. v. Hopkins, 47 Ill. 529. And it is fortunate for the people this power is so restricted. If, in the face of this law, a board of directors can lawfully contract for building a school house, to cost six hundred dollars, the contract price of the one in question, what is to prevent them to contract for a structure to cost sixty thousand dollars, or any other sum, and draw their orders on the treasurer at ten per cent in payment? We know of no limit to their power.

. . . .

It is also urged by appellee that the school house was accepted by the directors who incurred the debt, and that school was kept in it. That does not legalize the act, or bind the tax-payers. The question here presented is a question of power, and no act of the kind set up can make it valid for any purpose. Nor can the beneficiary in this case resort to such acts in support of his claim. In the absence of power to do the act, there can be no innocent holder of this paper. He should have looked to the authority to make the contract in satisfaction of which the orders are drawn.

There is no ground on which a recovery can be had against this board of directors, the appellants.

Guides for Class Discussion

1. On what basis did the court arrive at its decision?
2. Was the rule laid down by the court equitable from the point of view of the contractor?
3. See *Sullivan* v. *School District, infra.*

*45. ". . . if a school board enters into a contract for the purchase
of school property which it had authority to make and the contract
is unenforceable because of some irregularity in the making of
it, the board may later ratify it"* (p. 7).

SULLIVAN V. SCHOOL DISTRICT,
39 Kan. 347, 18 P. 287 (1888)
(Decided by the Supreme Court of Kansas)

[This was an action to recover from a school district money owed
a materialman by a contractor who had absconded from the state
before the building for which he had contracted with the board
had been completed. The district completed the building and had
since occupied it. When the district refused to pay the materialman,
he brought this action. The board contended there could be no
recovery because the original contract with Eley, the contractor who
absconded, was not made in the manner prescribed by statute. It
had been made between Eley and a single member of the board,
although there was evidence tending to show that the board had
later ratified it. The real issue before the court was whether the
board could legally ratify such a contract which had been irregularly
made.]

VALENTINE, J. . . .

It must be remembered that the case was disposed of in the court below
merely upon a demurrer to the plaintiffs' evidence. Hence the only real
question for us now to consider is merely whether that portion of the
evidence most favorable to the plaintiffs tended to prove the aforesaid
ratification and confirmation or not, and not whether the whole of the
evidence in the case in fact proved the plaintiffs' case or not. . . . It is
admitted that the original contract with Eley was, at the time it was
made, void, for the reason that it was not made by the entire school
board, but only by a portion thereof. . . . But it is claimed by the plaintiffs
that the evidence introduced in the court below tended to show a ratification of the contract by the entire school board, and also by the entire
school-district. We think such a contract might be ratified, and might be
made binding upon the school-district. . . . We think the evidence tended
to prove that the contract was ratified by the school board, and also by
the school-district. . . . We might say, however, that almost everything
seems to have been done irregularly in that school-district. In some cases
the director ignored both the other members of the school board, and

generally the director and the treasurer ignored the clerk, and the clerk often failed to make entries. It seems that the school-district and its officers permitted, and perhaps even authorized these irregularities; and hence the courts should not construe these irregularities, or these separate acts of the separate members of the school board, too critically.

Guides for Class Discussion

1. Are you in agreement with the court? Give reasons.
2. See *School Directors* v. *Fogelman, supra.*
3. Do you think that the history of irregularities mentioned influenced the court's decision?

46. *"Formal action to ratify is not necessary; ratification takes place when a board so acts that its action is incompatible with any other assumption than its intent to ratify"* (p. 7).

FRANK v. BOARD OF EDUCATION OF JERSEY CITY,
90 N.J.L. 273, 100 A. 211 (1917)
(Decided by the Court of Error and Appeals of New Jersey)

[This was an action to collect from a school board for work done and materials furnished it by unauthorized agents. The contracts for such purchases were of a type that the district had the authority to make. The agents in question were a supervising architect and a vice principal of a high school. In making the purchases, the agents were only doing what had been permitted " 'for a number of years.' " Plaintiff had furnished other materials and done other work for the board under similar circumstances, and the board had always paid when billed. The board, in this case, did not deny the authority of the agents in question until three years after the last work had been performed. The lower court ruled in plaintiff's favor, and the board appealed. The higher court affirmed the decision of the lower court. In so doing it held there was an implied agency and that ratification could be implied from the board's acts.]

BLACK, J. . . .

.   .   .   .

In the case under discussion, the School Law of the State . . . provides that the board of education in a city school district such as Jersey City is vested with the power of making contracts in and by its corporate name and by section 50 every such board shall have the supervision, control, and management of the public schools and public school property in its district. It may appoint a superintendent of schools, a business manager, and other officers, agents and employes, as may be needed. Section 52 provides the board may at any time order repairs to school buildings to an amount not exceeding $500, may authorize the purchase of supplies to an amount not exceeding $250, without advertisement. Section 72 provides for a business manager, who shall supervise, if there be one, the construction and repair of all school buildings, and shall report monthly to the board of education the progress of the work; that repairs not exceeding the sum of $100 may be ordered by the business manager, and repairs not exceeding the sum of $500 may be ordered by the committee of the board having charge of the repair of school property, without the previous order of the board and without advertisement. In this statute, as will be seen, there is express authority for the appointment of an agent, a business manager. The term is immaterial. A supervising architect or vice principal might just as well be called an agent or business manager. . . .

The literature of the law of agency is rich in adjudged cases. . . . The agency may be implied from the recognition or acquiescence of the alleged principal as to acts done in his behalf by the alleged agent, especially if the agent has repeatedly been permitted to perform acts like the one in question. . . . So ratification may be implied from any acts, words, or conduct on the part of the principal which reasonably tend to show an intention on the part of the principal to ratify the unauthorized acts or transactions of the alleged agent . . . , provided the principal in doing the acts relied on as a ratification acted with knowledge of the material facts. . . . The rule is particularly applicable, where it appears that the principal has repeatedly recognized and affirmed similar acts by the agent. . . . So a municipal corporation may ratify the unauthorized acts and contracts of its agents or officers which are within the scope of the corporate powers, but not otherwise. . . .

Guides for Class Discussion

1. What line of reasoning did the court follow in arriving at its decision? Are you in agreement with the court's thinking? Give reasons.
2. The court noted that the board knew that the materials were

furnished and the work done about the time when this happened. Do you think this affected the result? Why?

3. What limitation to the general rule, that ratification may be implied from the board's actions, did the court recognize?

47. *"It is difficult to determine what constitutes substantial performance of a building contract but the courts are agreed that there is . . . substantial performance . . . [if] the building is such as to accomplish the purpose for which it was built" (p. 8).*

State v. Goodman,
351 S.W. (2d) 763 (Mo.) (1961)
(Decided by the Supreme Court of Missouri)

[In Missouri a school board and a contractor, who had been awarded the contract for the construction of a combination gymnasium and music building, found it impossible to agree and litigation was resorted to. The contractor had substantially completed the building when the district took it over. It had been using the building for approximately three years when this action was brought. The real question before the court was the amount due the contractor by the board. In its decision the court commented on the meaning of "substantial completion" or "substantial performance" as it outlined the method for determining the amount due the contractor at the time of final settlement.]

Storckman, Judge.

. . . .

. . . the evidence showed that on September 6, 1957, plaintiff's architect, the defendant, and the attorneys for the parties went through the building together and that the architect "made up a list of what remained to be done." This was referred to as the "punch list" and was introduced in evidence as plaintiff's Exhibit Y. No evidence was offered, however, as to the cost of completing the items on the punch list. As to these items the opinion states, 336 S.W. 2d loc. cit. 101: "As of September 21, 1957, the architect compiled a list of items (a punch list) necessary to finally complete the building in accordance with the plans and specifications. Aside from the defective roof (eliminated by the stipulation of the parties) the larger of this long list of items was '5 doors missing,' replacing certain other doors with doors of another type wood, painting in places, grouting certain windows and numerous other small items. The district was entitled to a completed building, including these items, and the list establishes that the building was not complete. Nevertheless the architect had certified, as the contract contemplated, that there was 'substantial completion' of the building. . . ."

Paragraph III of plaintiff's pleading having been voluntarily dismissed, the items on the "punch list" so far as the record shows, were the only ones needed to make the building conform to the plans and specifications. The architect had certified to the board that the building was substantially complete as of May 21, 1957. *The building was substantially complete when it had reached the stage in its construction when it could have been put to the use for which it was intended* even though comparatively minor items remained to be furnished or performed in order to make it conform to the plans and specifications of the completed building. . . . [Emphasis supplied.]

Guides for Class Discussion

1. What constitutes "substantial performance"?
2. Compare this decision with the one rendered in *Dodge* v. *Kimball, infra.*
3. What was meant by the statement "The district was entitled to a completed building . . ."?

48. "A school board may not refuse to accept a schoolhouse if the contractor has acted in good faith and substantially performed his contract . . . [but, in such a case] the board will be required to pay the contractor [only] the contract price, less deductions to cover omissions in performance" (p. 8).

DODGE V. KIMBALL,
203 Mass. 364, 89 N.E. 542 (1909)
(Decided by the Supreme Judicial Court of
Massachusetts, Berkshire)

[This was an action to recover payment on the balance of the contract for the construction of a building. Plaintiff became a bankrupt and never completed the building. There were at least 10 different particulars in which the contract was not performed. By agreement of all parties concerned, the matter was referred to a referee whose determination of matters of fact was final, but his decisions of law were subject to review by the courts. He ruled that plaintiff was not entitled to recover, and plaintiff appealed his decision to the courts. In making its ruling, the court was forced to consider whether there had been substantial compliance and whether defendant could be required to pay for that part of the contract which was performed.]

KNOWLTON, C. J. . . .

. . . .

It is to be noticed, first, that the question whether there was a substantial performance of the contract is to be determined in reference to the entire contract. . . . The referee might well find that the plaintiff failed to perform the contract substantially, in view of all his departures from it. . . . The validity of the finding must be determined in reference to all the facts of the case. But as the referee indicates that this breach is the principal reason for his decision we will consider this branch of the case by itself.

Formerly it was generally held in this country, as it is held in England, that a contractor could not recover under a building contract, unless there was a full and complete performance of it, or a waiver as to the parts not performed, and that he could not recover on a quantum meruit after a partial performance from which the owner had received benefit, unless there had been such subsequent dealings between the parties as would create an implied contract to pay for what had been done. . . . But in most of the American states a more liberal doctrine has been established in favor of contractors for the construction of buildings, and it is generally held that if a contractor has attempted in good faith to perform his contract and has substantially performed it—although by inadvertence he has failed to perform it literally according to its terms—he may recover under the contract, with a proper deduction to the owner for the imperfections or omissions in the performance. . . . It would seem that in cases of this kind, while the plaintiff recovers under the contract, not the contract price, but the contract price less the deduction, he ought to aver, not absolute performance, but only substantial performance of his contract and a right to recover only the balance after allowing the owner a proper sum for the failure to do the work exactly in the way required. . . . The rule very generally adopted is that, to entitle the plaintiff to recover, he needs to show only that he proceeded in good faith in an effort to perform the contract, and that the result was a substantial performance of it, although there may be various imperfections or omissions that call for a considerable diminution of the contract price. The reason for this construction of such contracts is in part the difficulty of attaining perfection in the quality of the materials and workmanship, and of entirely correcting the effect of a slight inadvertence, and the injustice of allowing the owner to retain without compensation the benefit of a costly building upon his real estate, that is substantially, but not exactly, such as he agreed to pay for. In none of the courts of this country, so far as we know, is the contractor left remediless under conditions like those above stated. The recovery permitted is generally upon the basis of the contract, with a deduction for the difference between the value of the substantial performance shown and the complete performance which would be paid for at the contract price.

Guides for Class Discussion

1. While this case did not involve a school building, did this have any effect on the decision?
2. How did the court arrive at its decision?
3. Are you in agreement with this decision? Give reasons.

49. *"Even though a school building has been accepted and paid for, it has been held that a school board may sue the contractor for defective performance"* *(p. 8).*

Rubino v. Board of Trustees,
12 Cal. Rptr. 690 (1961)
(Decided by the District Court of Appeal,
Third District, California)

[This was an action brought by a contractor, who constructed a school plant and playground, to recover for additional work performed by him in order to remedy a defect. The defect was discovered after the contract had been completed and the work accepted by the board. The cost of repairing the damage was $973.40. It was to collect this amount that this action was brought. The plaintiff contended that, when the board accepted the building it discharged him from all obligations, even though the contract had been defectively performed; and that the board was liable for the cost of repairs. The board contended otherwise. The trial court ruled in favor of the board and against the contractor. On appeal, its decision was upheld by the higher court.]

SCHOTTKY, Justice.

.   .   .   .

The trial court found that "the proximate cause of the damage to the southwest corner of the playground area was the overflowing of the water from the ditch due to the inadequacy of the eight-inch well casing to carry the flow of the ditch." The court found further that the school district "ordered Plaintiffs to repair the damage aforesaid in January, 1969 [sic], maintaining that this damage was caused through the fault of the Plaintiffs; that Plaintiffs disclaimed any responsibility for the damage but, without admitting liability or responsibility and because it was raining and in order to avoid additional damages, the Plaintiffs caused repairs to be made." The repairs cost $973.40 and this action was brought to recover this amount. As stated recovery was denied.

Appellants contend that acceptance of the work precludes recovery on behalf of the school district for any later discovered defects. Appellants rely on cases such as City Street Improvement Company v. City of Marysville, 155 Cal. 419, 101 P. 308, 23 L. R. A., N. S., 317, and Hagginwood Sanitary District v. Downer Corporation, 179 Cal. App. 2d 756, 3 Cal. Rptr. 873. Both involved contracts with provisions to the effect that the work was to be done under the direction and to the satisfaction of an engineer. Both held that acceptance by the engineer precluded recovery for any defective work except if fraud were proved. In Hagginwood Sanitary District v. Downer Corporation, supra, the court stated at page 760 of 179 Cal. App. 2d, at page 876 of 3 Cal. Rptr: "It is the rule in this state that the decision of an engineer or superintendent approving or disapproving the work as performed under a contract is in the absence of fraud, bad faith or mistake conclusive and binding on the parties where the contract either expressly provides that it shall be final and conclusive or in plain language shows that it was the intention of the parties that the person to whom the question is submitted shall be the final arbiter of it. Brown v. Aguilar, 202 Cal. 143, 259 P. 735. . . ."

We do not believe that the decisions relied upon by appellants are determinative of the instant appeal. The appeal is on the judgment roll and the contract is not a part of the record. The question of whether the acceptance operated as a discharge of the defectively performed contract was a question of fact for the trial court to resolve . . . , and we must assume that the evidence supports the findings and judgment of the court denying recovery.

The judgment is affirmed.

Guides for Class Discussion

1. Do you think this decision is equitable? Give reasons.
2. Had the defect been discovered as much as five or ten years after the building had been accepted, do you think the court would have held as it did? Why?

50. "Authority to build schoolhouses carries with it by implication authority to require a contractor to whom a building contract is let to give a bond guaranteeing the faithful performance of the contract and the payment for all labor and materials used in the construction of the building" (p. 8).

BOARD OF PRESIDENT AND DIRECTORS OF THE ST. LOUIS PUBLIC SCHOOLS V. WOODS,
77 Mo. 197 (1883)
(Decided by the Supreme Court of Missouri)

[When a contractor, who had agreed to construct a schoolhouse, failed to perform the duties required of him under the contract, the school board brought this action to collect from his sureties. Specifically, it was charged that the contractor failed to pay all just claims of sub-contractors and materialmen, items covered by the bond. Defendants argued that the bond, in so far as it authorized plaintiffs to bring this suit, was void because plaintiffs were only authorized, by statute, to contract for the construction of the building and payment therefor. The main question before the court was the authority of the board or district to require a bond in the absence of statute so authorizing it to do.]

MARTIN, C. . . .

. . . .

I am unable to adopt the conclusion reached by the learned counsel for the appellant, to the effect that the bond now sued on was beyond the powers of the board to accept, or that it "is repugnant or inconsistent with the objects of its creation." By the act of incorporation, the board is vested with "the charge and control of the public schools and all the property appropriated to the use of public schools within said city." It is also empowered "to do all lawful acts which may be proper or convenient to carry into effect the object of the corporation." . . .

The board of public schools certainly has the power to build school houses. It has the right to make contracts with contractors for the erection of school buildings. And as germane to these powers, I think it has the right like any other proprietor, to exact conditions from its contractors, which shall tend to secure and pay off the material men and laborers, who unquestionably contribute most to the erection of such buildings. Viewed from the narrow standpoint of private economy, this must be the cheapest way to erect such costly and commodious structures. Otherwise as the statutes furnish no security to material men or laborers in the mechanics' lien law, as against the board, on account of its being a municipal corporation, they will be compelled to add something to the materials and labor going into the school buildings, on the well known principle which prevails throughout the business world, that high prices and high interest always attend bad security. In a wider sense, I think, the bond is germane to the corporate objects of the school board. . . . I must decline to hold that the school board in the conduct of its business transactions ought to be controlled by such a phlegmatic sense of justice toward its builders, as the learned counsel for the appellants think so appropriate to it as a public corporation. The object and purpose of the bond being entirely within the powers of the board, and the board being constituted the trustee of an express trust in the bond, the right to sue on it ought not to be questioned.

Guides for Class Discussion

1. Is this decision equitable? Give reasons.
2. By what line of reasoning did the court arrive at its decision?

51. ". . . *the obligation of a surety on a bond to insure the performance of a building contract is measured by the terms of the contract; but where the liability in the contract is broader than in the bond, many courts have held that the bond is the measure of the surety's liability*" (p. 8).

DUNLAP v. EDEN,
15 Ind. App. 575, 44 N.E. 560 (1896)
(Decided by the Appellate Court of Indiana)

[This was an action by a contractor against a sub-contractor and his surety upon a performance bond. In this case, the contract provided that the sub-contractor would be responsible for paying for any and all materials, but the bond contained no such provision. The question before the court was whether surety's liability was governed by the terms of the contract or the bond.]

Davis, C. J. . . .

. . . .

The rule is that where a written instrument is the foundation of a pleading, and is made an exhibit, its statements will control the allegations of the pleading. . . . Therefore, in determining the liability of the sureties in this action, we are governed by the terms and conditions of the bond, and not by the allegations in relation thereto in the complaint. The contention of counsel for appellant is that the contract and bond, having been executed contemporaneously, are treated as one instrument, and that the sureties on the bond are bound for the performance of all the terms and conditions of the contract. Assuming that the bond and contract should be read and construed together, it does not follow that the obligors on the bond are liable for all the debts contracted by Eden in the execution of the contract. They are only bound to the extent that they guarantied the payment of such debts. . . . In this case, under the terms and conditions of the contract, Eden was to complete the work, pay for the work and material, and indemnify Waggener against loss, etc.; but, under the terms of the bond, the obligors were bound only that Eden should complete the work, and indemnify Waggener. In other words, as before observed, there is no provision in the bond that Eden shall pay for the work and material. There is no general condition in the bond that Eden shall in all things fully keep and perform the contract between himself and Waggener. There is no provision therein of similar import. The language of the bond is clear, plain, and explicit, and there is no averment that there was any mistake in drawing the bond, by reason of which the condition that Eden should pay for labor and material was omitted. It is a familiar rule that where a bond appears to be complete and perfect on its face, with conditions fully expressed, a new condition, in the absence of mistake, cannot be added.

Guides for Class Discussion

1. While this decision was rendered in a case brought by a contractor against a sub-contractor, do you think the court would have followed the same rule had the case involved a school district and a contractor instead? Give reasons.
2. What implications does this case have for school administration?

52. ". . . *contracts for suretyship will be construed . . . strictly against a surety for pay*" (*p.* 8).

Phoenix Indemnity Co. v. Board of Public Instruction,
114 So. (2d) 478 (Fla.) (1959)
(Decided by the District Court of Appeal of Florida, First District)

[This was an action against a contractor and his surety on a performance bond for the purpose of recovering unpaid insurance premiums for workmen's compensation, public liability, and property damage insurance taken out by the contractor. The contractor was required by statute to carry the insurance and to furnish the bond. In fact, the contract was made a part of the bond. In addition to the conditions prescribed by the statutes, the bond was also conditioned to guarantee the payment of "all bills for '*services* furnished to the principal in connection with the contract.'" The question before the court was whether the surety, under the bond, could be held liable for the cost of the insurance mentioned. The court held it could.]

Sturgis, Judge.

. . . .

While this is a case of first impression in Florida, it is the general rule that whether a surety for compensation will be held liable for unpaid insurance premiums depends strictly upon the terms of the bond as construed in the light of applicable statutes.

. . . .

In the last case [McCrary v. Dade County, 8 Fla. 652, 86 So. 612, 614] it was held that the phrase "supplying labor and materials in prosecution of the work" is not limited in meaning to the structure, building or thing produced in which the labor or material must actually enter and become an integral part. Adhering thereto, we hold that the liability of the surety for the insurance premiums involved in this suit must be construed in accordance with the terms and qualifications of the formal public works contract for the performance of which the bond was given, or in the light of the special circumstances under which the insurance was furnished. And as the bond in suit is conditioned to pay bills for "services" and to complete all "work comprehended by the contract free and clear of all liens for labor or materials, or otherwise," we are persuaded that it contemplates performances and a guaranty beyond those specifically required by F.S. Section 255.05, F. S. A.

Contracts of suretyship for compensation are to be construed most strongly against the surety and in favor of the indemnity which the obligee has reasonable grounds to expect. They are regarded in the nature of an insurance contract and are governed by rules applicable to such contracts. The maxim that "sureties are favored in the law" has no application to contracts of suretyship by one engaged in the business for hire. The provisions of the bond should be considered as a whole and given that effect which was logically intended by the parties as shown by the entire instrument. . . .

Guides for Class Discussion

1. Compare this decision with the one rendered in *Dunlap, Eden, supra.*
2. On what basis did the court arrive at its decision?

53. *"When the bond is given by a surety company for pay, the bond is interpreted as are other contracts with a view of giving effect to the true meaning of the parties" (p. 8).*

BLYTH-FARGO CO. v. FREE,
46 Utah 233, 148 P. 427 (1915)
(Decided by the Supreme Court of Utah)

[In an action to recover on a bond given pursuant to a contract to construct a tunnel, the primary question before the court related to the interpretation of the bond. In arriving at its decision, the court gave considerable attention to how a bond should be interpreted.]

FRICK, J. . . .

. . . .

Counsel for appellant insist that the bond in question is an indemnity bond pure and simple, and was intended to indemnify and save harmless the company for any damages it might suffer in case the contractor did not, in the particulars specified in the bond, comply with its conditions.

. . . Respondent contends that, inasmuch as appellant copied a certain provision contained in the contract into the bond, it was bound to copy it correctly, or suffer the consequences. . . .

. . . Taking the bond as it is written, and under the pleadings and evidence, we must arrive at the intention of the parties from the bond as written, can the respondent sustain this action? Counsel contend that in view that the appellant is engaged in the business of furnishing such bonds for profit, and for the reason that it determines upon the language and phraseology that is used therein, therefore such bonds are to be liberally construed in favor of the beneficiary. A number of cases are cited in support of the contention. While some courts use the expression that bonds given under such circumstances are to be liberally construed in favor of the beneficiary, yet that is not precisely what the courts mean. The rules or canons of interpretation which are resorted to by the courts to aid them in arriving at the meaning or intention of any written document, instrument, contract, or statute, are precisely the same in every case. Where, however, the intention or meaning is once ascertained, then the application of the contract to the subject-matter is in certain cases and under certain circumstances perhaps more liberal than under others. It has many times been decided that sureties are favorites of the law, and that "the contract of a surety is strictissimi juris, and it is not to be extended beyond the express terms in which it is expressed." . . . This is all that the courts mean when they use the somewhat loose expression, which they sometimes do, that the contract of a surety is to be "strictly construed." Moreover, what is meant by the expression that the surety or indemnitor who executes such bond for profit does not come within the rule of strict construction is that, as against such surety or indemnitor, when the meaning or intention of the parties to such an instrument is once ascertained the bond will be applied neither strictly nor liberally, but with the view of effectuating the object or purpose for which it was given. Although a surety under such a bond is entitled to have the meaning and intention of the parties determined by the same rules that the meaning and intention of parties to other instruments are determined, yet in case of an ambiguity in the language used, or, if a doubt arises by reason of the use of a particular term or phrase, the doubt may be, and usually is, resolved against the surety for profit, whereas it may be, and usually is, otherwise as against a voluntary surety.

Guides for Class Discussion

1. While this case did not involve a school district, do you think the court would have followed a different line of reasoning if it had?

2. Compare this decision with the one rendered in *Dunlap* v. *Eden, supra;* with *Phoenix Indemnity Co.* v. *Board of Public Instruction, supra.*

54. "Under the common law it was originally held that any change in a contract without the consent of the surety released the surety from all liability" (p. 8).

INDEPENDENT DISTRICT OF MASON CITY V. REICHARD,
50 Iowa 98 (1878)
(Decided by the Supreme Court of Iowa)

[This was an action to recover on a bond to secure the performance of a school-building contract entered into by a contractor with a school board. Some time after the signing of the contract the board and the contractor entered into a new agreement altering the terms of the original contract. When the contractor failed to complete the project, this action was brought to collect from him and his surety. The surety contended that, because the contract for which the bond had been given was altered, it was relieved of all liability, and the court agreed.]

DAY, J. . . .

. . . .

This contract was signed by Jacob Reichard [contractor] and by the board of directors of plaintiff, and attested by their secretary. There is no proof that the sureties upon the bond assented to this contract, and it is not claimed that they ever did assent thereto. The changes made by this agreement are material. By the original contract defendant Jacob Reichard was to have twenty thousand dollars in bonds as soon as he gave bond, with sureties, for the proper performance of his contract. Under this supplemental agreement no payment was to be made until twenty days after the agreement was signed, and then only twelve thousand dollars was to be paid. Of the balance, the payment of six thousand dollars was to be postponed until the walls of the building were completed and ready for the joists; one thousand dollars was not to be paid until the building was accepted; and the remaining one thousand dollars was to be allowed to the school board for negotiating the bonds. We think it is very clear that these changes operated to discharge the sureties upon the bond.

"Any alteration, however *bona fide*, by the creditor and the principal, without the assent of the surety, of the terms of the original agreement, so far as they relate to the subject-matter in respect of which the surety became responsible for the principal, will exonerate the surety." Chitty on Contracts (11th Ed.), 776. "And this doctrine seems to hold, although the new terms thus substituted vary only in a slight degree from those of the original agreement." Id., 777. In regard to this principle, in *Miller* v. *Stewart*, 9 Wheat., 680, it is said: "It is not sufficient that he" (a surety) "may sustain no injury by a change in the contract, or that it may even be for his benefit. He has a right to stand upon the very terms of his contract, and if he does not assent to any variation of it, and a variation is made, it is fatal."

Guides for Class Discussion

1. Do you think this decision was equitable? Give reasons.
2. Had surety approved the changes in the contract, do you think the court would have held it liable on the bond, or would it have required a new bond?
3. The court noted that the changes made in the contract were "material." Do you think it would have held as it did had they been "immaterial"? Give reasons.

55. ". . . *it is generally held that [if any change in a contract is made without the consent of the surety for pay] the surety will be relieved entirely only if the change in the contract increases his liability materially; and, if the change is not great enough to relieve the surety entirely, he will be relieved pro tanto—i.e., to the amount of his extra obligation*" (p. 8).

MARYLAND CASUALTY CO. v. EAGLE RIVER UNION FREE HIGH SCHOOL DISTRICT,
188 Wis. 520, 205 N.W. 926 (1925)
(Decided by the Supreme Court of Wisconsin)

[The nature of the action and issue before the court is clearly stated in the quotation which follows.]

OWEN, J. . . .

.   .   .   .

The appellant claims, generally, that it was discharged from its obligation by reason of breaches of the contract on the part of the school district in paying out money contrary to the provisions of the contract. It claims that money was paid to the contractor in violation of the contract provision that payment should be made only once a month, and then only upon architects' certificates, and only to the extent of 90 per cent. of the material and labor entering into the construction of the building. It also claims that a complete new contract was made between the school district and the contractor in March, 1923, when the school district agreed to advance money in the manner set forth in the statement of facts, to enable the contractor to prosecute the work of construction. . . .

At the outset of our consideration of this case it is well to have in mind the general principles of law touching the liability of paid sureties upon bonds of this nature, at least so far as they can be invoked to work a discharge of the surety. It is thoroughly established by the decisions of this court that contracts of this kind, entered into for a consideration by surety companies engaged in such business, are in effect contracts of insurance, and the contracts are not to be construed according to the rules of law applicable to the ordinary accommodation surety. . . . Sureties were favorites of the common law, because their liabilities were gratuitously assumed. The rules and principles of the common law declaring the rights and liabilities of sureties were developed in an atmosphere surcharged with sympathy for the surety. Accordingly it was held that any conduct prejudicial to the surety resulted in the total discharge of the surety from any liability. . . .

The number of cases coming to the courts, in which paid sureties are urging their complete discharge by reason of some infraction of the contract on the part of the indemnified, suggests that a more specific rule concerning their rights and liabilities be stated. . . . While the contract between the parties should govern their rights and liabilities, such contract should no longer be construed strictly in favor of the surety. This has often been declared. It would seem too, that not every circumstance prejudicial to the interests of the surety should work a total discharge of the surety, without any reference or consideration to the extent to which the interests of the surety were in fact prejudiced by such circumstance. In other words, a paid surety should not suffer damage by breach of any duty or obligation resting upon the indemnified; but neither should the surety be permitted to profit thereby. If the breach on the part of the indemnified results in damage to the surety, the surety should be compensated for such damage, but no further.

. . . We must not be understood as saying that there can be no conduct on the part of the indemnified which will result in the absolute discharge of the paid surety; but we say that, as a general proposition, considerations of justice are fully met when the surety is recouped to the extent of the losses actually sustained by reason of misconduct on the part of the indemnified.

Guides for Class Discussion

1. Do you think the rule laid down by the court is equitable? Give reasons.
2. On what basis did the court arrive at its decision?
3. See *Dunlap* v. *Eden, supra;* and *Phoenix Indemnity Co.* v. *Board of Public Instruction, supra.*

56. *"A surety who gives a bond guaranteeing the performance of a building contract and the payment for labor and materials will not be relieved of his obligation to laborers and materialmen by any alteration in the original contract to which they did not give their consent"* (p. 9).

UNITED STATES FIDELITY & GUARANTY CO. v. CICERO SMITH LUMBER CO.,
290 S.W. 307 (Tex.) (1927)
(Decided by the Court of Civil Appeals of Texas, Amarillo)

[This was an action by a lumber company against a contractor and his surety for an unpaid bill for lumber used in the construction of a schoolhouse. The bond in question was made for the use of those furnishing material under the contract. The bonding company denied liability on several grounds, one of which was based on the contention that, inasmuch as the board had not retained 20 per cent of the contract price until the building was completed, as it had agreed to do, surety was relieved of its liability. The question before the court was the effect of the alteration of the original agreement, to which the materialman did not consent, on the liability of surety.]

HALL, C. J. . . .

.   .   .   .

The first proposition urged in the brief is that sureties upon a contractor's bond for the construction of a public school building are discharged where the trustees of the district fail to retain 20 per cent. of the contract price until after the building was completed, as required by the contract. We overrule this contention, for the reason that the bond recites that it was made for the use of all persons who might furnish material under the contract, and further provides that any one furnishing material could sue upon the bond, though not specifically named as an obligee therein. In answer to special issue No. 2, the jury found that the payment of more than 80 per cent. of the contract price had been made by the school trustees without the knowledge and consent of the lumber company. While such excess payment by the trustees would have released the sureties from all liability to the owners of the building, the rule is otherwise as to parties furnishing material to be used in the building. The rule is that, where the obligation names materialmen and laborers as obligees, the sureties are not discharged from liability to them by reason of the owner having made payments in violation of the bond, unless such obligees knew of such violation at the time they furnished the material.

Guides for Class Discussion

1. How do you think the court would have ruled had the school district, instead of a materialman, been the complainant?
2. Do you think this decision is equitable? Give your reasons.

57. *"Where there is evidence . . . that the contractor intended to give a statutory bond, the terms of the statute will generally be read into the bond and the surety will be held liable to pay for labor and materials"* (p. 9).

Collins v. National Fire Insurance Company of Hartford,
105 So. (2d) 190 (Fla.) (1958)
(Decided by the District Court of Appeal of Florida, Second District)

[At issue in this case was the question of whether a performance bond that did not specifically contain the statutory provision that it guaranteed payment to all persons supplying labor, material, and supplies to the contractor or subcontractors, protected laborers and materialmen. The court held that it did, on the ground that the bond should be construed in light of the law or statute requiring it and the purpose it is supposed or expected to accomplish.]

KANNER, Chief Judge.

.   .   .   .

The purpose of the provision contained in section 255.05, that a contractor shall promptly make payments for labor, material, and supplies, is to protect laborers and materialmen whose labor and material are put into public buildings or projects on which they can acquire no lien. A contractor's bond should be construed in the light of this section and must be supposed to accomplish its purpose. . . .

.   .   .   .

In the case of the City of Ocala for Use of Standard Oil Co. v. Continental Casualty Co., 1930, 99 Fla. 736, 127 So. 326, 77 A. L. R. 8, the action was against the contractor's surety and the contractor to recover for material and services rendered to the contractor in connection with street improvements, which action involved the question of the sufficiency of the bond. In that case, it is stated, quoting from 127 So. at page 328:

"There was no duty or obligation of the surety company to enter into the bond that the statute requires the contractor to execute 'before commencing' the 'public work.' If a surety company executes a penal bond purporting in terms or in substance or by sufficient reference to be in accordance with or for the purpose of complying with the requirements of the statute in cases of such contracts, as to 'additional obligation that such contractor shall promptly make payments to all persons supplying him labor, material and supplies used directly or indirectly in the prosecution of the work provided for in the contract,' the surety company will be liable as provided by the statute. . . ."

.   .   .   .

In the Ocala case the bond contained no language to meet the requirement to protect the laborers or materialmen, nor was there language in the contract to fulfill this deficiency. However, it is clearly indicated that where a surety company executes a penal bond which appears by sufficient reference to be in compliance with or for the purpose of fulfilling the statutory bond conditions designed to protect laborers and materialmen in cases of public improvement, the surety company will be liable as provided by the statute.

Where a written contract refers to and sufficiently describes another document, that other document or so much of it as is referred to, may be regarded as a part of the contract and therefore is properly considered in its interpretation. Also where a contract expressly provides that it is subject to the terms and conditions of other contracts which are definitely specified, such other contracts must be considered in determining the intent of the parties to the transaction. . . . The bond here specifically referred to and described the contract and expressly stated that the contract was annexed to it. The contract was so annexed. Under the stated principles, we hold that the language contained in the surety bond here sufficiently by reference incorporates into the bond the language of the contract hereinabove quoted from article 7.

Guides for Class Discussion

1. Compare this decision with the one rendered in *Tennessee Supply Company* v. *Bina Young & Son, infra.*
2. Are you in agreement with the line of reasoning adopted by the court? Give reasons.

58. *"Where there is evidence . . . that the contractor intended to give a statutory bond, . . . [some] courts interpret the bond strictly and will not read the terms of the statute into it"* (p. 9).

Tennessee Supply Company v. Bina Young & Son,
142 Tenn. 142, 218 S.W. 225 (1919)
(Decided by the Supreme Court of Tennessee)

[This was an action against a contractor and the security on his bond by a materialman to collect for materials furnished the contractor and used in the construction of a school building. The bond had apparently been taken to meet the statutory requirement, although the bond itself was not as broad as the statute. The question before the court was whether the bond should be interpreted strictly, or whether the terms of the statute should be read into it. The court held that the bond should be interpreted strictly.]

McKinney, J. . . .

. . . .

Later . . . [the school commissioners] charged that the contractors had not erected said building according to contract, and asked that they be decreed damages on account of such breach.

They also charged in said cross-bill that it was the intention of the parties to have said bond drawn so as to comply with chapter 182 of the Acts of 1899, and prayed that said bond be reformed accordingly.

.   .   .   .

We will first dispose of the assignments of error made by the school commissioners, the first of which is as follows:

"The court erred in refusing to decree a reformation of said bond so as to expressly show that said contractors were to pay the materialmen and furnishers for the material used in construction of said building, and to have said bond so expressly provide."

.   .   .   .

A bond was executed by the contractors and delivered to Mr. Graf, the architect. This bond is not embodied in the transcript in this cause, and the record does not show the provisions and conditions thereof. However, Mr. Graf, acting for the school board, declined to accept said bond, but submitted a bond which had been prepared by his attorney, and which was executed by said contractors and their surety without any change or alteration. Mr. Graf testified that he had never heard of the act of 1899, and hence he could not have had same in mind.

The surety company executed the bond prepared by the obligees, and without any agreement as to the terms and conditions to be contained therein further than appears by the bond itself, which was prepared by the agent of the obligees, and it would be unfair and unjust to the surety company to reform the bond so as to make it different from the one which the parties agreed upon.

The second assignment of error is as follows:

"The court erred in holding and decreeing that said bond is not in compliance with chapter 182 of the Acts of 1899, and that therefore said surety company is not liable on said bond for the material and labor that went into the Jellico school building, and in failing to grant appellants a decree against said surety company for the aggregate amount of the decree in this cause for materials furnished Bina Young & Son by materialmen, to wit the sum of $3,980.77 and interest thereon and costs of the cause."

It has been held by this court that a bond of this character does not comply with chapter 182 of the Acts of 1899. . . .

.   .   .   .

It is apparent in this case that the bond was executed for the benefit of the owner, and not for the benefit of the laborers and materialmen, and since complainants are not parties to the bond, nor beneficiaries thereunder, they have no cause of action against the surety on said bond, and the chancellor was correct in dismissing that part of their bill.

Guides for Class Discussion

1. Compare this decision with the one rendered in *Collins* v. *National Fire Insurance Company of Hartford, supra.*
2. See *Green Bay Lumber Co.* v. *Independent School District, Infra.*
3. What line of reasoning motivated the court?

59. *"Where a contractor agrees to provide the labor and materials used in the construction of a school building and gives a bond to guarantee that his contract will be performed, he does not definitely agree to pay for the labor and materials, and there is no right of action against his surety"* (p. 9).

GREEN BAY LUMBER CO. v. INDEPENDENT SCHOOL DISTRICT,
121 Iowa 663, 97 N.W. 72 (1903)
(Decided by the Supreme Court of Iowa)

[This was an action by one who furnished materials to a contractor engaged in constructing a school building against a contractor and the sureties on his bond. The contract provided that the contractor would furnish labor and materials. "The sureties demurred on the ground that the bond was executed solely for the benefit of the district." The trial court sustained the demurrer, and its action was upheld on appeal.]

LADD, J. . . .

The sole question on this appeal is whether the bond executed by the contractor to the school district was also intended for the benefit of subcontractors furnishing labor and materials. If not so intended, the sureties are not liable, and the demurrer was properly sustained. It will be observed that the contract merely required Weaver to provide materials and perform the labor, but contains no stipulation in relation to the payment therefor by him. A condition for compliance therewith imposed on the bondsman no liability to the subcontractors. . . . The bond exacted first the erection of the building in compliance with the contract, and its "delivery free from any liens or claims of any kind." As no liens or claims might be asserted against the building, the sureties were safe in pledging that it should be without them. . . . Certainly an agreement to discharge them cannot be implied from a contract that a building shall be delivered clear of liens and claims, and it is inferred therefrom that payment shall be made of claims which could in no event be asserted against the building. . . . Neither the bond nor the contract in suit exacts of the contractor payment of labor or materials used in the building. . . . by no fair construction can the language be said to bind the contractor to pay any liens or claims whatever. It binds him to do no more than repay the district what it has been compelled to pay for the purposes mentioned. A careful reading of the bond leads to the inevitable conclusion that the sole object had in its execution was the indemnity of the school district. Not having been executed for the benefit of the labor and material men, they cannot recover thereon. . . .

Guides for Class Discussion

1. Do you think the rule laid down by the court in this case is equitable?
2. See *Tennessee Supply Company* v. *Bina Young & Son, supra.*
3. How could sureties have been made liable for labor and material?

60. "Where a contract . . . provides that the board retain each month a certain percentage of what is due the contractor in order to insure the completion of the building, and the contractor defaults, the contractor's surety has a claim on the retained percentage superior to that of laborers and materialmen or of a bank to which the contractor has assigned his rights to the retained percentage" (p. 9).

Levinson v. Linderman,
51 Wash. 855, 322 P. (2d) 863 (1958)
(Decided by the Supreme Court of Washington, Department 2)

[In this case a contractor defaulted and his surety completed the contract at a cost of $89,159.70. The district still owed—*i.e.*, it had retained—$62,200.29. This it deposited in the court's registry. Plaintiff and others had obtained a judgment against the contractor for $3,413.54. In addition, a bank had loaned the contractor $15,000 upon his promissory note, secured by the assignment of a progress payment. The question before the court was the distribution of the amount retained by the district. The trial court subordinated the claims of the surety to the judgment creditor and contract creditor just mentioned, whereupon surety appealed. The court, here, reversed the lower court and held that where the surety completed the contract, the funds retained by the board belonged to the surety by right of subrogation.]

Foster, Justice.

. . . .

The bank could not fail to know that the contract was for the construction of school buildings and that a performance bond was required by RCW 39,08.010 at the time of the execution of the contract. Inquiry would have shown that the contract prohibited the assignment in question, and that the school district had the right under the contract, in the event of the contractor's default, to complete the buildings and to use all sums unpaid for that purpose.

. . . .

The funds distributed by the judgment belong to the surety and not to the contractor, and, therefore, the bank acquired nothing by the assignment because the contractor had nothing to assign. . . .

.   .   .   .

There is another compelling reason for reversal. This is not a case of priorities between assignees under separate assignments of moneys belonging to the contractor, for the surety completed the buildings at a cost of $89,159.70, with only $62,200.29 remaining unpaid on the contract, and the deposited funds belong to the surety by right of subrogation.

The school district had the right to complete the work in any way it chose and to use the unpaid balance therefor. When the surety completed the construction, it was subrogated to the rights of the school district to the unpaid balance, and all of the funds in the court's registry belong to it.

.   .   .   .

The judgment must be reversed because the assignment was prohibited by contract and is, therefore, void, and the funds involved are those of the surety by right of subrogation. Upon the contractor's default, the school district had the right to apply the entire unpaid balance to the completion of the construction, and the surety on the performance bond completing the contract is subrogated to all its rights.

The judgment of respondent Osina under the writ of garnishment falls for the same reason, for at the time of the service of the writ, October 24, 1955, more than a year after the contractor's default and the completion of the work by the surety, the school district was not indebted to the contractor; hence, the respondent Osina obtained nothing by the garnishment.

Guides for Class Discussion

1. What is meant by the "right of subrogation"?
2. Are you in agreement with the court's reasoning? Give reasons.

61. "It is commonly held that a school district will not be held liable for failure to take a bond conditioned to pay for labor and materials even though a statute requires that such a bond be taken" (p. 9).

FREEMAN v. CITY OF CHANUTE,
63 Kan. 573, 66 P. 647 (1901)
(Decided by the Supreme Court of Kansas, Division No. 1)

[In this action an attempt was made to hold a municipality liable for loss sustained by one as the result of furnishing material to a contractor engaged in the construction of a public building. The municipal officers, in spite of a statute that required all persons who contracted to construct public improvements to give a bond, failed to require the contractor in question to provide the bond. On the ground that, because the district failed to obey the law, it should be held liable for loss sustained by a materialman, this action was brought. The court held the district not liable and ruled against the plaintiff.]

GREENE, J. . . .

. . . There are two kinds of duties which are imposed upon a municipal corporation. One is of that kind which arises from the grant of a special power, in the exercise of which the municipality is a legal individual. The other is of that kind which arises or is implied from the use of political rights under the general law in the exercise of which it is a sovereign. The former power is quasi private, and is used for private purposes; the latter is public, and used for public purposes. . . . In the exercise of its quasi private or corporate power a municipality is like a private corporation, and is liable for a failure to use its power well, or for an injury caused by using it negligently. In building its waterworks, gas, electric light plants, sewers, and other internal improvements which are for the exclusive benefit of the corporation, it is in the exercise of its quasi private power, and is liable to the same extent as are private corporations. . . . But in the exercise of the political or public power conferred upon it as an arm of the state for the benefit of all the people its officers, although appointed or elected by the city, paid and subject to be discharged by it, are not the agents of the municipality, but of the state, and the corporation is not liable either for their misfeasance or nonfeasance. . . .

The duty of taking the bond provided for in the statute . . . is not imposed upon the corporation. It is not taken for the benefit of the corporation or its inhabitants, but is for the benefit of any person who shall perform labor or furnish material to the person or persons who contracts with a public officer to construct any public improvements, whether such person be a resident of the city or elsewhere. The duty is a public one in the interest of the public, imposed by statute upon public officers, and with which the corporation in its private capacity has no concern.

Guides for Class Discussion

1. Compare this decision with the one in *Plumbing Supply Co.* v. *Board of Education, infra.*
2. The defendant in this case, it will be noted, was the city of Chanute. Do you think the court would have held the same had it been a school district? Give reasons.
3. Are you in agreement with this decision? Give reasons.

62. *"Where the statutes require a school board to take a bond conditioned to pay for labor and materials . . . members of the board will not, as a rule, be held personally liable for failure to take such a bond . . . ." (p. 9).*

PLUMBING SUPPLY CO. V. BOARD OF EDUCATION,
32 S.D. 270, 142 N.W. 1131 (1913)
(Decided by the Supreme Court of South Dakota)

[This was an action questioning the personal liability of school board members for failure to take a bond when the statute made it the duty of all public corporations to require that a contractor, when awarded a contract for the construction of a school building, put up a bond conditioned for the payment of labor and materials. The court here held that the school board members could not be held liable individually for their failure to obey the statute.]

McCoy, J. . . .

We are of the opinion that there is not now and never was any common-law liability against officers of this class, individually, for neglect to perform official duties. At common law the king could not be sued without his consent. Neither could any officer who represented the king. The same principle has been applied to the sovereign power of the state in this country. Members of a board of education fall within this class of officers who represent the king or who represent the sovereign power of the state in a public official capacity. Liability for negligence and suit therefor against the individual officer can only exist by virtue of an express statute creating the individual duty of such officer, and also authorizing the maintenance of a suit for failure to perform such duty. No such individual duty, as charged in the complaint, has ever been imposed upon such officers as members of a board of education as individuals, in this state. From a close reading of chapter 245, Laws 1909, it will be observed that the duty to take a contractor's bond, as alleged in the complaint, is imposed on the corporation only, and not on the officers thereof as individuals. . . .

. . . .

School districts are state agencies exercising and wielding a distributive portion of the sovereign power of the state, and the officers of school districts are the living agencies through whom the sovereign state act is carried into effect. A school district officer in the performance of his duties acts in a political capacity, as much so as the Governor of a state, and is not liable for negligent acts of omission occurring in the performance of such political or public duties, unless the sovereign power of the state has authorized and consented to a suit for such negligence. Now, in the matter of letting building contracts for the repair or construction of a public school building, and the taking of a contractor's bond, we are of the opinion that the members of a board of education act in a public and political capacity, as an agent of the state, in the carrying out of a portion of the distributed functions of state government, and are not liable to suit for negligent acts of omission, unless the state has by express statute consented to such suit. It therefore necessarily follows that there is no common-law liability for such negligent acts as are complained of in this case against the members of the board of education, as personal individuals, or as officers composing the board, and that if any such liability exists at all it must be based upon statute.

Guides for Class Discussion

1. Compare the decision in this case with the one in *Warren* v. *Glens Falls Indemnity Co., infra.*

2. Compare this decision with the one in *Freeman* v. *City of Chanute, supra*.
3. Which of these cases represents the "best" law? Give reasons.

63. *"Where the statutes require a school board to take a bond conditioned to pay for labor and materials . . . members of the board will [in some jurisdictions] . . . be held personally liable for failure to take such a bond" (p. 9).*

WARREN v. GLENS FALLS INDEMNITY CO.,
66 So. (2d) 54 (Fla.) (1953)
(Decided by the Supreme Court of Florida,
Special Division B)

[This was a suit against sureties on the official bonds of members of a County Board of Public Instruction, to recover loss incurred by plaintiff who furnished materials to a contractor on a school construction project and was unable to collect therefor. He based his claim on the ground the board failed to perform a ministerial duty, required by statute, of taking a bond from the contractor to guarantee payment of labor and materials. The lower court held against plaintiff, who appealed. The higher court reversed the lower court. It held the duty of taking the bond was mandatory and failure to follow the statute made the board members individually liable in tort.]

DREW, Justice.

. . . .

Section 255.05, Florida Statutes, 1951, F. S. A., has been on the statute books for many years. It was placed there to protect laborers and materialmen who incorporate their labor and materials in public buildings on which they can have no lien. This section is extremely broad in its scope. It concerns itself with all public buildings and we find nothing in the School Code to even infer that it was not intended to apply to school buildings. On the contrary, section 237.31(4) can, and should, be construed to make this section, 255.05, a part thereof because, in section 237.31(4) it is expressly provided that the contractor *shall* provide bond "in such amount and for such purposes as [*shall be*] *prescribed by law* . . . ." (Emphasis supplied.) . . .

It is urged upon us by defendants below that the statute, 255.05, *supra*, does not place a ministerial duty on the board to require the bond; they say:

". . . ; it does not say that the board of public instruction shall require a person entering into a contract to execute a particular type bond. It was incumbent upon the contractor to furnish the proper bond and of course the school board would have approved of his bond if the bond furnished had complied with the regulations as set out in the School Code. . . ."

We wholly disagree with this argument. The provision in the statutes that the bond shall be required before commencing work is patently and clearly the same as saying that the school board shall see to it that the contractor does not begin work until the bond is executed, posted and duly approved. Only it would have such authority. The purpose is quite obviously to protect those who incorporate their labor or material in the structure. If there is any doubt as to the duty of the board in this respect, such doubt is completely dissipated by the concluding two sentences of the section making it the duty of the public body to furnish a copy of such bond to interested persons.

It is therefore our conclusion that it was the mandatory duty of the school board members to see to it that the bond required by said section 255.05 was posted before work was commenced; that the duty to do so was ministerial; that the failure to do so was a breach of the duty to faithfully perform the duties of the office and that persons suffering loss because thereof had a remedy against such board members individually in tort.

Guides for Class Discussion

1. Compare the holding in this case with that in *Plumbing Supply Co.* v. *Board of Education, supra.*
2. Which case represents the better law? Give reasons.
3. Compare this case with *Freeman* v. *City of Chanute, supra.*

SELECTED BIBLIOGRAPHY

1. Edwards, Newton. *The Courts and the Public Schools,* rev. ed. Chicago: University of Chicago Press, 1955.

2. Garber, Lee O. (Ed.) *Law and the School Business Manager.* Danville, Ill.: The Interstate Printers & Publishers, Inc., 1957.

3. Garber, Lee O. *Yearbook of School Law.* "School Property." Danville, Illinois: The Interstate Printers & Publishers, Inc., annually since 1950.

4. Hamilton, Robert H. and Paul R. Mort. *The Law and Public Education,* rev. ed. Brooklyn: The Foundation Press, Inc., 1959.

5. Hamilton, Robert R. and E. Edmund Reutter, Jr. *Legal Aspects of School Board Operation.* New York: Bureau of Publications, Teachers College, Columbia University, 1958.

6. Punke, Harold H. *The Courts and Public-School Property.* Chicago: University of Chicago Press, 1936.

7. Reutter, E. Edmund, Jr. *Schools and the Law.* ("Legal Almanac Series," No. 17.) New York: Oceana Publications, Inc., 1960.